Out
of
Ashes

Dr. Keith Phillips

World Impact Press
2001 S. Vermont Avenue
Los Angeles, California 90007
AREA CODE NOW) 735-1137
323

This book is dedicated to all my co-laborers who contributed to and prayed for its completion, especially Tim Goddu, Beth Gould, Steve King, Susie Krehbiel, Nic Nelson and Jim Parker. They labored with me above and beyond the call of duty to communicate that God can bring a crown of beauty *Out of Ashes*.

Except where otherwise indicated, scripture quotations are from: *Holy Bible: New International Version®. NIV®.* Copyright ©1973, 1978, 1984 by The International Bible Society. Used by permission of Zondervan Publishing House. All rights reserved.

The characters, settings and events in this narrative are true. To protect the privacy of the individual, fictitious names are sometimes used.

Published by World Impact Press
A Division of World Impact, Inc.
Los Angeles, California 90007
Printed in U.S.A.

ISBN 0-9655553-0-5

Contents

Foreward

Here is a book *of* hope, *on* hope. And it's written by a man who *brings* hope everywhere he turns.

I got to *know* Keith Phillips long after I met him. The meeting was formal, short and socially appropriate. I met a man who was the founder of an inner-city ministry called World Impact. I was polite in my acknowledgment, and even said I would like to have him come to our church sometime and talk about his ministry.

He did.

But when he came, I became *far* more interested—compellingly stirred—by the *people* of World Impact, including Keith and his wife Katie. There was plenty to be impressed with by World Impact's *work*, but I was overwhelmed by their *workers*. It's hard to know what quality to put first in assessing them:

- They are committed to the inner city, and don't just serve there—they go and *live* there, 24 hours a day!
- They are caring, compassionate and truly Christian—without an ounce of empty religionism, but with tons of love.
- They are intelligent, resourceful, creative and wise—a better bunch couldn't be found from the graduates of any of the colleges or universities from which they've nearly all come.
- And they are spiritually *driven*; consumed by the call of their Lord, Jesus Christ, and focused on winning souls to Him.

This analysis could go on, but much more would begin to sound as though a multitude of Mother Teresas have arrived at World Impact's address. And that's about the size of it. These people are just plain *real*, with a selfless devotion to reach and help others, to teach kids how to live, to show teens how to succeed in work, to recover the broken and introduce them to the Redeemer and—most of all—to demonstrate His *reconciling love* at our society's centers where hate, racism, violence and murder have reigned too long.

And behind this troop with such commitment, there are two men: (1) **The Man** Above All, named Jesus of Nazareth, whose heartbeat sets the *pulse* of World Impact's ministry; and (2) Keith Phillips, a man possessed by **The Man**, whose passion sets the *pace* for World Impact's advance.

There's nothing exaggerated in these words. This isn't sentiment: just fact. And that's why the pastors and elders, with the entire assembly that I serve at The Church On The Way, join me in continued belief in and support of World Impact's ministries across the United States. I've served on the World Impact Board for four years now, and I've learned two things about this organization beside what I've said above: *there's no ministry more prudently frugal, and none more passionately faithful.*

So here's *hope*—a whole bundle of stories that will make your heart sing like Isaiah's, when he wrote of Messiah's mission and its fulfillment through His people:

> "No longer will violence be heard in your land, nor ruin or destruction within your borders...[because] The Spirit of the Sovereign Lord is on me...to preach good news to the poor...to bind up the brokenhearted...to comfort all who mourn...
>
> **To bestow on them a crown of beauty instead of ashes...they will be called oaks of righteousness, a planting of the Lord, FOR THE DISPLAY OF HIS SPLENDOR!"**
>
> --Isaiah 60:18; 61:1-3

Dr. Jack W. Hayford
The Church On The Way
Van Nuys, California

October, 1996

Preface

Envision this with me. It is the turn of the twenty-first century. A reporter from the *Los Angeles Times* has been given the assignment of covering the miraculous transformation that has swept the inner cities of America. Her banner headline reads:

"Inner Cities Reborn: Urban Renewal Becomes A Reality"

The reader is astounded by the news of justice and peace in neighborhoods once demeaned as "ghettos." He is heartened by the reports of excellent schools, flourishing commerce, widespread home ownership, community responsibility and declining crime. This unbelievable change rivals the fall of the Berlin Wall and the end of Communism.

The studious reader is amused that sociologists, anthropologists and politicians seem dumbfounded at how a community could be transformed in such a few years, especially since this radical redirection has not emanated from some master political initiative, nor from a major philanthropic thrust.

The article reports, "Few observers can explain the origins of this urban renaissance, although most participants consistently credit a carpenter from Nazareth, born about 3 B.C., as the inspiration and guiding light."

The reader discovers that every urban neighborhood, numerous high-rises, most housing projects and many inner-city apartments have churches led by community residents. These houses of worship have sprouted up like California poppies in the desert. Each one is beautiful by itself, but when viewed together they form a carpet that reflects the magnificence of its Creator.

The front page story concludes, "Today the American inner city is one of the most splendid mosaics in human history—a culturally, racially and linguistically diverse community, where residents live at peace with each other and with their God."

Such an article seems fanciful in light of the despair all around us. But the Lord of history is in control. In more than 30 years of urban ministry, I have learned a great deal about God's optimism and compassion for the inner cities of America. *Out of Ashes* is a personal chronicle and a prophetic word. I write from my perspective as a middle-class Anglo coming to grips with late twentieth-century American urban problems, the greatness of God, and how His Bride, the Church, can bring beauty out of ashes.

I invite you now to take the first steps with me through a minefield of controversial issues, which must be navigated if we are to reach the pinnacle of unity in Christ, and witness our cities reborn. *Out of Ashes* explores the roots of the poor and oppressed in America and explains God's design for urban renewal. It is not a plan of commercial centers, industrial parks and greenbelts, but of His highest, most precious creation: people. World Impact's vision and strategy for church planting is an effective Christian response to the hopelessness among the urban poor.

"To bestow on them a crown of beauty instead of ashes...
They will renew the ruined cities that have been devastated for generations" (Isaiah 61:3-4).

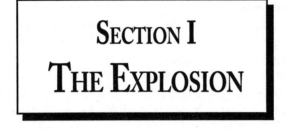

SECTION I
THE EXPLOSION

"When he opened the Abyss, smoke rose from it like the smoke from a giant furnace" (Revelation 9:2).

"There was shooting back there now, and on either side of me they were throwing garbage cans, bricks and pieces of metal into plate glass windows. I moved, feeling as though a huge force was on the point of bursting."
--Ralph Ellison, *Invisible Man*
(New York: Signet, 1947), 476.

Chapter I

The Tinderbox Ignites:
The 1992 Los Angeles Riots

Wednesday, April 29, 1992, was a sultry day in Los Angeles. I spent the afternoon in a budget meeting, planning for the next fiscal year. About two o'clock my wife, Katie, phoned to tell me that the jury had returned innocent verdicts in the trial of the officers charged in the Rodney King beating.

I had previously contemplated the possibility of a violent reaction to a "not guilty" verdict. After I prayed that people would stay calm, I returned to strategizing for the growth of our inner-city ministry.

A couple of hours later a colleague's wife phoned, telling us that the news media was reporting a minor disturbance at the corner of Florence and Normandie. Once again I heard that datum but could not bring myself to face the likelihood of an explosion. Certainly the police, who had had days to prepare for the announcement of the verdict, would calm any random disorder.

Around 6:30 p.m., along with co-workers Don Allsman and Al Ewert, I walked to the parking lot behind World Impact's corporate offices. As we were about to leave I said to Al, a dear friend of mine for over 20 years, "I think you ought to be cautious going home. Why don't you take the freeway instead of the side streets?"

Al normally traveled south on Normandie Avenue to his home in South-Central Los Angeles. That night he took my advice, got off the Harbor Freeway at Florence, drove a few blocks and stopped at a red light behind a vehicle driven by another Anglo. Suddenly, three or four gang members, bricks in hand, approached the car in front of Al. When Al saw that the man ahead of him was in serious danger, Al instinctively reached for his car door handle in order to jump out and help.

As Al's hand touched the handle he glimpsed another group of angry young men coming toward the stopped cars. Al immediately realized that he, as well as the man ahead of him, was in deep trouble.[1]

Al bowed his head, thinking of his bride of 17 months who was pregnant, and told the Lord, "I am ready to come home, but it sure would be great to see the birth of my first child."

When Al opened his eyes and looked up, he watched as his prayer was answered. The traffic signal turned green and a police officer drove through the intersection. That was miraculous, since police were virtually absent from the streets of South Central that evening. The crowd dispersed. The man in front of Al sped off, and Al shakily drove the few remaining blocks home.

Deja Vu

In 1965, when I started our ministry in the Watts community of Los Angeles, I witnessed an astounding event—armored personnel vehicles rolling down 103rd Street, flanked on both sides by well-armed guardsmen in full battle fatigues with bayonets fixed.

The scene could have been clipped from news coverage of a third-world coup. I had no context in which to place this violent outburst. I half expected a Hollywood director to yell, "Cut—print it," but this was not staged. It was real!

I never thought I would see a recurrence of that event—certainly not in Los Angeles. Tragically, 27 years later, I watched history repeat itself.

---

[1] Al had driven into the heart of the most deadly and destructive riot in American history. *Inside the Los Angeles Riots*, (Institute of Alternative Journalism, 1992), 10.

The 1992 riots on the streets of Los Angeles were the worst domestic disturbance in America since the Civil War. Mobs looted and burned 10,000 buildings without impediment from the police. Fires soared hundreds of feet into the air. Fifty-eight people died; 2383 were injured. Over $1 billion in property was damaged; $500 million in wages were lost and 3700 businesses were destroyed.[2]

As I watched the destruction all around, despair overwhelmed me. I had an empty, powerless feeling in my stomach. An angry mob ran down Vermont Avenue, where our office is located, breaking into countless buildings, looting and torching as they went. There was no authority to phone—we could do nothing to stop the violence destroying our community.

People who had put their security in anything, or anyone, other than Almighty God discovered abruptly that their trust had been misplaced.

---

[2] The hardest hit area in the Watts riots also bore the brunt of the 1992 Los Angeles riots.

	1965 Watts riots	1992 Los Angeles riots
Deaths	34	58
Injuries	1,032	2,383
Arrests	3,953	17,000
Buildings burned	600	10,000
Property damage	$183 million	$1 billion
Days of rioting	6	3
LAPD officers	934	5,000
Guardsmen	13,900	9,975
Federal troops	—	3,313
Other agencies	719	1,950
California Highway Patrol	60	2,323

(Los Angeles Times, 1 May, 1992)

Chapter II

Extinguishing The Flame
A Messenger From The Lord

By Friday, day three of the 1992 Los Angeles riots, I wondered if God was even in control.

For a brief moment that afternoon, I was heartened when I heard the words over the phone, "I think we can help your work, Keith." This well-meaning Washington bureaucrat continued, "If you submit a budget for recreational leagues, I believe we can get a grant." My encouragement was short-lived.

I looked out my office window. Smoke was rising over my city, which appeared to have been bombed. It was a war zone. The streets were deserted. This was no time for football, baseball, soccer or "midnight basketball."

Then another government agency phoned, offering housing to victims in the riot area who had been burned out of their homes. Washington did not understand that primarily businesses and shops had been the targets; few residences were destroyed.

I asked if the available government housing could be used for the homeless who had been without shelter for months. The bureaucrats did not think so (the plight of the homeless had to have been directly connected to the riots), but they pledged to get back to me. They never did.

Political expedience, it seemed, motivated Washington's compassion. Every politician wanted to be the first to respond to "the riots." However, few cared to address the shameful despair of the hurting long-term victims, much less the root causes of the riots.

I fully expected government promises. Prompted by the riots, President Clinton proposed Empowerment Zones to help blighted urban areas and promised Los Angeles $100 million to revitalize the riot-ravaged community.[1] HUD Secretary, Henry Cisneros, said that the 100 square miles of riot-damaged South-Central Los Angeles had stimulated the drafting of the Empowerment Zone legislation.[2] Ironically when the funds were distributed to several inner cities, Los Angeles was passed over.[3]

I knew that the aftermath of the riots would be packed with investigations, studies and commissions. Reports and recommendations would be made. Even before any groups were convened or findings released, I knew—we all knew—what their conclusions would be: our inner cities needed better schools, more job training, greater incentives to work, stronger families and improved police-community relations. We all could have predicted what would happen: more reports, more studies—little action—no difference.[4]

Didn't anyone understand or care? Wouldn't anyone help?

A few hours after the phone calls from the government, Dr. Jack Hayford, a member of World Impact's Board and pastor of the 8,000-member Church On The Way in the San Fernando Valley, phoned to ask how I was doing. I confessed my discouragement.

Pastor Jack said that God had given him a verse for me. I listened as he quoted Isaiah 61:3 which promises that the Lord will bring a crown of beauty out of ashes. I could see the ashes, smell the residue and sense the destruction. I could hardly imagine a crown of beauty.

---

[1] *Los Angeles Times*, 27 May, 1993: B3.
[2] *Governing Magazine*, Mar., 1994: 32-36.
[3] *Los Angeles Times*, 20 Dec., 1993: A1.
[4] Art Buchwald bemoaned the government providing aid to several foreign countries, such as Russia, but not helping troubled Los Angeles. *Los Angeles Times*, 27 Sept., 1995: C2.

Pastor Hayford expressed his belief that God would transform Los Angeles' ashes into hope. He knew that God would bring many people to Himself, and cause others to look to Him, as a result of this tragedy.

I started to reflect. The hopelessness we were experiencing could lead to revival. When people realized their precarious situation, maybe they would turn to the Lord, the only Rock of their salvation.

God's Word, through Pastor Jack, began to bolster my spirit. I shared his inspiration with our inner-city missionaries, and through them, with those we serve.

Almost immediately, the Lord started to do great and mighty things. We began to see the opportunity the riots provided for Christian witness. Pastor Jack was wise to speak God's Word first.

On Saturday, Pastor Hayford phoned again. His church was about to meet for their weekly worship services. He asked how his congregation could most appropriately respond to the riots.

I explained that a tremendous number of people to whom we minister depend upon social security and welfare checks for their existence. Since the riots erupted at the end of the month, their checks were not delivered. Post offices had been burned. Thousands of our neighbors were without money to purchase food. Children and the elderly were going hungry.

Furthermore, most of the prime targets of the looters had been stores, crippling the food supply in South-Central Los Angeles. Many who had money had no transportation to get to the grocery stores outside their neighborhood, where food was available. The lack of food was a serious crisis. By providing food, in the name of Christ, the Church could display tangible compassion in a critical situation.

Dr. Hayford listened.

On Sunday afternoon, Pastor Jack called once more. I could tell he was struggling to hold back the tears. As he related what had happened, we both rejoiced. In response to Jack's plea, his people had brought over $50,000 worth of food to church, and a member of his congregation had offered to transport the food to our facilities and to other churches and ministries in South Central.

Jack then told me that God had led him to take an offering for the ongoing physical needs of people in our riot-ravaged city. To his amazement, members gave $200,000 to purchase food and supplies for the riot victims in the name of Jesus.

I was overwhelmed by the spontaneous and generous response of God's people![5]

My astonishment continued on Monday morning. As I looked out of my office window, trucks and cars packed with food, money and volunteers from congregations all over Southern California, began arriving. Pastors, elders and church leaders had collected food and funds to provide nourishment and hope for the hurting people in the inner city of Los Angeles.

I could hardly contain my emotions as I witnessed the generous outpouring of Christian love, just when some had given up hope.

South Coast Community Church sent a $10,000 offering to purchase food, but where could we buy the food since the grocery stores had been looted? Who would do the purchasing? Should we pull our missionaries away from the needy families they were assisting and turn them into shoppers? How could we honor, in an immediate and decisive fashion, the request of the Christians who sent this generous check?

Within moments, faculty and staff from Azusa Pacific University arrived unexpectedly. Their president, Dr. Richard Felix, had sent them to help us display practical Christian love. We gave them the money. They bought the food, sorted it and assisted our missionaries in distributing it to many families we knew were in need.

Mrs. Kennedy lived on a fixed income. She had no transportation and no food. When we gave her food in Jesus' name, she was so thankful she helped us deliver food to most of the

---

[5] I later thanked The Church On The Way for their faithful generosity over the years by presenting them with an oak tree, symbolizing their ministry of planting oaks of righteousness, a display of God's splendor, in the inner cities (Isaiah 61:3).

elderly and shut-ins in her community. Our neighbors were especially thankful for "box milk" (no refrigeration required), fruit, vegetables and bread.

Thuan Vuong, a former World Impact missionary, then studying at seminary, returned to his old ministry neighborhood with ice to preserve food. There had been no power for four days.

Other volunteers came with shovels and brooms in hand and joined our missionaries and their neighbors in cleaning up devastated businesses and heaps of rubble. Some merchants wanted to pay us; many stood in disbelief as Christian volunteers explained that they served in the name of Jesus. Their actions showed strong support for, and solidarity with, the community.

Pastor Hayford's response to the riot was impeccably biblical. First, Jack *declared* God's Word. Nothing fills the empty void in your stomach like manna from heaven. Then, he *demonstrated* the Word that he declared. Joined by thousands of other Christians, Pastor Jack and his congregation preached a powerful message of hope and reconciliation through their *declaration* and *demonstration* of the gospel. God was bringing a crown of beauty out of ashes, but there were still a lot of ashes.

Chapter III

The Sparks

The 1992 riots were ignited by the jury verdict following the March 3, 1991 roadside beating of Rodney King. A few days after the riots subsided, I spoke at a university, urging Christians to become involved in our inner cities. Many students asked what had caused the riots. Was it clearly and solely a case of police brutality, or was it an over-reaction on the part of African Americans?

I responded that the riots were not primarily an outburst of Black hostility, although years of racial prejudice and discrimination were involved: more Latinos than African Americans were arrested for civil disobedience and looting. Portraying the riots as a Black versus police confrontation oversimplified the matter and distorted the facts reinforcing prejudice and racism.

Most inner-city residents know from personal experience that police brutality happens regularly in their neighborhood. This used to be hard for me to believe, since I grew up in a White community, confident that the police protected and served citizens. If I had a flat tire, the police would help. In an emergency, they would be there. If someone had threatened to harm me, they would protect me. The police would stand up for my civil rights.[1]

---

[1] Even George Holliday, the man who videotaped the King beating, had a reservoir of good will toward the Los Angeles Police Department. He said, "I feel bad for the police department. I think the beating was out of line, but I've never had a bad experience with them." Beth Shuster, "Man Who Taped King Beating Defends LAPD," *Los Angeles Times*, 10 Mar., 1996: B1, B4.

However, after ministering in the inner city for thirty years, I now know that some peace officers abuse their authority.[2] Sadly, a few of our missionaries have experienced this first hand. One of our staff was rudely pulled out of his car, thrown over the hood and searched because he looked out of place in the neighborhood. How could the police have known he was a visiting missionary, not a drug dealer?

Who could forget the sickening audio tapes of radio calls from Rodney King's arresting officers to their station, bragging about beating up another "trophy"? This warped conversation was indefensible.

Many observers wondered why people in South-Central Los Angeles did not riot when the Rodney King beating video was first aired on television. Certainly residents had a reason to demonstrate their disgust and impatience with a police force that, in their eyes, had a dual standard of law enforcement.

I believe the residents of South Central realized they finally had ironclad proof of police abuse against minorities. It could not be hidden. After all, the entire world had viewed the videotape. And so the people of South Central determined to let the justice system expose the truth.

The community was confident. A guilty verdict was a foregone conclusion. How could this blatant display of excessive force be rationalized away? Anything short of a guilty verdict would defy logic and justice.

---

[2] The Los Angeles Police Department uses force freely. In 1992, Los Angeles officers shot 52 suspects, killing 25 of them. The city paid more than $19.6 million in compensation in 188 cases of civil wrongdoing alleged against LAPD officers. Most of these settlements were in cases that the City Attorney did not want to take to trial.

In one case, a White motorcycle officer shot to death a Black tow-truck driver who posed no threat but refused to stop. The officer has a history of misconduct including three suspensions in six years, and his action was found to violate LAPD policy by Chief Willie L. Williams and the Police Commission. But the incident was deemed poor judgment and, unlike the officers who beat King, this motorcycle cop faces no criminal charges. This shooting was not on videotape for all the world to see. Lou Cannon, "Not an Open-and-Shut Case," *The Washington Post*, 21 Mar., 1993: C7.

Imagine, for example, a social worker threatening to take away our 16-year-old son, David, claiming that he is malnourished. Confidently we go to court bringing indisputable evidence that David is healthy: medical records—and 200-pound David!

The social worker offers no evidence, testimony or rebuttal, yet the judge rules that David is malnourished and takes him from us at once!

My immediate reaction is, "You are joking. Anyone with common sense would know David is healthy—and certainly not under-fed." The judge's irrational, incompetent and unfair decision *could* force us to lose respect for him and respond decisively—even if others saw our actions as illegal or irresponsible.

The verdict for the police officers' trial seemed to many city residents as irrational, incompetent and unfair as the judge's decision to remove David. Some reacted without much thought for law or responsibility. Others reasoned that tyrannical oppression demands a radical reply—like the righteous rebellion of the Boston Tea Party.

In spite of those feelings, most urban residents did not participate in the riots. Many stayed in their homes in fear. Others were involved as Good Samaritans. One Black pastor nearly sacrificed his life trying to save White victims. Another African-American minister risked his life to rescue a Guatemalan man from certain death. Some Black men broke up fights and drove injured Whites to hospitals. The riots were condemned by at least 60% of Los Angeles Blacks.[3]

What caused the riots? No simple explanation could be found for this domestic explosion. But there were definitely more than two theories, and one's vantage point significantly influenced one's opinion.

African Americans

Some African Americans felt deeply betrayed when they heard the "not guilty" verdict, which implied that the officers who arrested Rodney King were within their legal bounds when

---

[3] Joel Kotkin, "Los Angeles' Engine of Growth," *City Journal*, Winter, 1993: 64-69.

they beat him to within an inch of his life.

The first to explode were a few gangsters, throwing rocks and bottles at anything in sight. Their violent outburst ignited the fire inside others, and thousands of people took to the streets.

Memories of prejudice, discrimination and injustice fueled the flame. Eighty-one percent of African Americans believed that the criminal-justice system was clearly biased against them. Sixty percent of Black Americans felt police brutality against minorities was excessive.[4] African Americans had experienced over 300 years of injustice, unfair trials and biased jurors. The system remained unchanged.

The fire was further fed by resentment toward foreigners. African Americans had paid dearly for their citizenship (working in slavery for generations). They were upset that new immigrants were taking over their neighborhood businesses. Blacks believed that White banks favored Koreans over African Americans when making loans.[5]

African Americans claimed that frequently they were judged to be criminals when they walked into a Korean's store.[6] Employees followed Blacks up and down the aisles, treated them with disrespect, and sometimes with disgust.[7] Many Korean stores, like most small inner-city retail grocers, were expensive and usually made a lot of money on liquor.[8]

The tragedy of Latasha Harlins was fresh in most people's minds. When this African-American teenager picked up a bottle of orange juice from a grocery shelf, the Korean store owner

---

[4] Only 36% of Whites think the justice system is racially biased, according to a USA Today poll. Seventeen percent of Whites think police brutality is excessive. Manning Marable, "Los Angeles Point of View" *Inside the Los Angeles Riots* (Los Angeles: Institute for Alternative Journalism, 1992), 82.

[5] Peter Kwong, "The First Multicultural Riots" *Inside the Los Angeles Riots*, 91.

[6] Nora Choi, "Between Black Rage and White Power" *Inside the Los Angeles Riots*, 95.

[7] The Korean-Black tension continues. Recently an African-American pastor was refused service in a Korean haberdashery for women, where he went to look for a hat for his wife. This led to a boycott of the Korean's store by their African-American customers. Both the African American and the Korean were Christians. Andrea Ford and Connie Kang, "One Incident Reverberates in Two Worlds," *The Los Angeles Times*, 15 Feb., 1996: B1-6.

[8] Kwong, 90.

thought the girl was going to steal it, pulled a gun and shot her in the back. This videotaped killing happened two days after Rodney King's beating. The Korean grocer was only given probation.[9]

How do you expect African Americans to respond? Isn't your 15-year-old daughter, sister or friend worth more than an $.89 bottle of orange juice? What is justice?[10] During the riots this underlying ethnic tension erupted into full-fledged attacks on Korean merchants in the inner city.

Korean Americans

The Koreans wondered how they were connected to, and why they were being punished for, a police beating in a Los Angeles suburb.[11] Many lower-income Koreans had made the difficult transition from Asia to Los Angeles, attracted by economic opportunity. Several had spent ten or fifteen years living together with three or four families in small residences, working long days to build businesses. One cheap way to start a family business was to open a liquor store in South Central.

Over the years, numerous Koreans had had their stores robbed, had phoned the police for help, but received little response unless someone had been killed. In despair, many merchants vowed, "No one else is going to steal from our stores. It is not right."

Several owners of small businesses armed themselves for protection—the security they felt they did not get from the police. During the riots, many stood on the roof of their stores and fired warning shots over violent crowds. They had learned from other owners, who had not armed themselves and had paid dearly.

A few months before the riots a Korean-owned store around the corner from World Impact missionaries, Rich and Lori

---

9   Kwong, 91.

10 Understanding the Riots Part 3: Witness to Rage, (Los Angeles: A *Los Angeles Times* Special Report, 13 May 1992), 37.

11 Latino and Asian merchants owned 85% of all businesses damaged by the riots. Joel Kotkin, "Los Angeles' Engine of Growth," *City Journal,* Winter, 1993: 61.

Reardon, had been robbed. Early in the evening, four Black men entered the store, stole money from Jack, the owner, then shot and killed him. Jack, a Christian, was well-liked by store patrons.

Against this backdrop, consider the Korean view of the Latasha Harlins tragedy. Latasha was the 15-year-old African-American girl, who walked into the Korean-owned Empire Liquor Market Deli on South Figueroa Street and took a bottle of orange juice. The owner, Soon Ja Du, said, "You have not paid." As Latasha turned around and started to walk out of the door, Soon Ja Du pulled a gun, shot the teenager in the back and killed her.[12]

Soon Ja Du was overworked, alone and afraid. Her insecurity and desire to control the situation led to an overreaction in the shooting. But, how often can you be robbed before finally defending your property? When peace officers fail to come to your aid, at what point do you take the law into your own hands?

Police Officers

On the other hand, if you had been a police officer trying to enforce the law and had chased Rodney King as he sped through Los Angeles County on an eight-mile, 100-mile-per-hour odyssey, avoiding five police forces from five different jurisdictions before finally being coerced to stop, you might have had even a different perspective.[13]

Two of King's companions immediately surrendered, but King, driving with a blood alcohol content more than twice the legal limit, resisted arrest. (One officer later sued King, claiming if he had not resisted arrest, there would have been no riots, and the police officer's life would not have been ruined.) Sergeant Stacey Koon fired four darts from an electric stun gun into King in a failed attempt to subdue the 225-pound suspect.

---

12 Understanding the Riots Part 3: Witness to Rage, (Los Angeles: A *Los Angeles Times* Special Report, 13 May 1992), 37.

13 "Free Stacey Koon," *The Wall Street Journal*, 4 Aug., 1995: A8.

King stood up and harassed the police. He mouthed off, behaved as if he were on P.C.P. (an hallucinogenic drug), and looked like he might charge. These officers knew that people under the influence of P.C.P. often exert super-human strength. When they tried to force King to the ground, he did not submit.

Would Rodney King physically assault the officers? Imagine their fear of debilitating injury or permanent physical pain. They technically followed police procedures (since the choke hold had been outlawed, an uncooperative, violent suspect who did not submit quietly was to have been subdued with a baton). Unfortunately, the police ultimately lost control and inhumanely beat King.

These officers had not been provided with sensitivity training or support groups in between arrests. How often had they been spit on? How many times had bricks crashed through their windshields? How frequently had they been called names unfit to publish?

Is it tolerable to be a victim of the people you are sworn to protect and serve?[14] Was the macho behavior of the police a cover for their fear and vulnerability? Or was it an expression of their frustration at the constant disrespect and outright hostility that they faced daily?

The Jurors

The citizens who were summoned to listen, deliberate and render a verdict at the Simi Valley trial lived under the burden of weighing the legality of the police officers' actions against the rights of the apprehended. Even though the judge's instructions to focus on the evidence led the jury to conclude that the

---

[14] Mr. King was awarded $3.8 million in damages. Since then Rodney King has been arrested at least five times—once for beating up his wife, twice for drunken driving and last month for felonious assault on a woman using a deadly weapon, that is, his car. According to a witness who called the police: "He was telling her to get out of the car, calling her names and it sounded like a struggle, and he was pulling her out, and I heard him strike her a few times. Then, he hit her with the car. She was like in mid-flight to the floor and he just went speeding around the corner." The police made their own video tape of the arrest. "Free Stacey Koon," Review and Outlook, *The Wall Street Journal*, August 4, 1995, A-8.

officers were within the legal letter of the law, the jurors must have thought that their verdict *might* spark a violent reaction.

The jurors had to consider a multiple-convicted felon who resisted arrest and fought with reckless abandon. Many LAPD officers live in the Simi Valley. They were neighbors, friends or at least acquaintances of the jury. And the jury instructions said that to convict they would have to determine that the officers intended to do King harm *before they stopped him*. Who was right? Who was wrong? Where was Solomon?

As a student at the University of California, Los Angeles, I learned that in American jurisprudence it is better for ten guilty people to go free than for one innocent person to be incarcerated. How do you balance the rights of a defendant against the potential of a riot?

How would it feel to sit on the Rodney King jury knowing that your name and address might be published in the *Los Angeles Times* or reported on television? What happens to the American judicial system if the fear of mob rule dictates verdicts?[15]

Hispanic Americans

Fifty-one percent of the people arrested in the riots had Hispanic surnames (compared to 13% Anglo and 36% Black). Many recent Central-American immigrants took things that did not belong to them because they got caught up in a carnival atmosphere with no police to deter them. For most of these opportunists, their unlawful actions appeared rooted in greed and pressure from mob frenzy, not racial injustice. A few regretted their looting and over the next several days anonymously returned stolen merchandise to retailers or churches.

Some Central Americans, who had fled coups d'etat in their homeland, participated in food looting out of fear, thinking that

---

[15] Virginia Loya, a member of the jury which acquitted the Los Angeles police officers accused of beating King, anguished that the acquittal sparked the riots. *Los Angeles Times*, 19 Nov., 1993: JJ5.

after the riots and looting there would be no access to food for weeks. It had happened to them before.

Thousands of second- and third-generation Hispanic Americans grimaced, realizing that they would be unfairly judged by the actions of their newer, less-connected brethren.

The majority of Latinos in Los Angeles are moral and productive citizens. They are less than half as likely as the general population to depend on welfare. A far greater percentage of Hispanics work than non-Latino Whites.[16]

Most of the Latino community was shocked by the ferocity of the riots and embarrassed by the thousands of Latino immigrants who joined in the looting, as many had no need to loot.

Raimundo Jimenez, President of the Hispanic Christian Communications Network and a member of World Impact's Board, publicly apologized on behalf of Hispanics at the summer 1992 *Love LA*[17] meeting at Hollywood Presbyterian Church. With tears in his eyes, Raimundo confessed that the majority of rioters were Hispanic and most of their involvement was sparked by opportunism.

Reporters

Like most Angelenos, I was riveted to my television set and my news radio stations during the riots. They were addictive— I could not turn them off. I watched new fires, additional looters, more deaths. I was not alone.

Larry Martin, a former Bible-club student from Watts, works in the transportation industry. He is an upstanding citizen who came home from work during the riots and watched his friends drive into the projects with new television sets, VCRs, stoves, refrigerators and anything else they could find.

Larry knew he should not steal, but the temptation was real. So he went inside his home and drew the curtains to avoid the obvious allure outside. But there, on his television screen, he saw more friends at a nearby store, taking anything they wanted.

---

[16] Joel Kotkin, 59.
[17] A regular gathering of hundreds of pastors, ministers and Christian leaders, who pray for Los Angeles.

One wonders how much less the riots would have expanded had the press not covered every detail, explaining exactly which stores were open for looting, where there were no police, or at which businesses police were sitting across the street in patrol cars watching, but not interfering with, the looters.

The media coverage of the riots blurred the line between reporting and entertainment. Were the press reports intended to inform the public, or to increase ratings? Whatever the intent, the result was a very well-informed body of looters. General Schwarzkopf could not have better coordinated their "intelligence gathering."

The press heralded their right to free speech and their obligation to report all the news; the city begged for restraint, fearing the result of throwing gasoline on an open flame. The public's right to know stood squarely at odds with their right to safety.

Summary

These six views are only a sample of the numerous perspectives people in the same city had about the circumstances that fostered the riots. I have not written about the harassed firemen, the frightened suburbanites, the innocent urban victims, the bewildered politicians or the concerned Christians.

But no matter what your vantage point—had Rodney King *never* been beaten, or had the jury *convicted* the four police officers—Los Angeles would still have been a tinderbox waiting to explode. The jury verdict after the King beating was simply the straw that broke the camel's back (and a camel can carry a lot of straw)!

SECTION II
CREATING
THE TINDERBOX:
THE CAUSES

"What caused the riots?" The question is hard to answer, given the conflicting views of Los Angeles residents. Some argue racial injustice or oppression was the stimulus; others blame the poor communication between the mayor and the police chief, leading to an understated response by police officers. In reality, the riot was only a symptom of a much deeper problem.

THE ROOT CAUSE OF THE RIOTS WAS THE *HOPELESSNESS* OF THE URBAN POOR, THE DISENFRANCHISED, THE ALIENATED.

For decades, the urban poor have been assured that things would get better for them. The Civil Rights Movement, the Great Society, Trickle-Down Economics and a plethora of public and private "promises" have offered them hope. While much has been gained in the last 50 years, particularly for African Americans, the full expectations envisioned by Martin Luther King, Jr., Lyndon B. Johnson and Ronald Reagan have not been realized.

Promises were made, expectations stimulated—and then, hope faded.

When people are told to defer their dreams—year after year, generation after generation—frustration mounts. Cynicism grows. Deep-seated anger expands into fully-developed resentment. "Hope deferred makes the heart sick" (Proverbs 13:12).

When Rodney King was, in effect, publicly beaten, and then "the system" set his tormentors free, accompanied by overwhelming public sentiment in favor of the officers' release (led by the police chief), it became too much for many people. The huge number of participants in the riots illustrated how widespread the alienation was. Too little hope, deferred too long, resulted in explosive behavior.

While not sanctioned by society, the riots provided an emotional outlet for years of frustration with virtual immunity from retaliation for the great pleasure of getting something for nothing. Masses felt they had little to lose, leading to the rationale, "I might as well loot and take everything I can—if the system can be this corrupt and violent, then so can I."

The rioters were disproportionately young and poor. Many were street-gang members. Once the police were out of the picture—barricaded in their stations, protecting firemen or not reacting to crime—gangs were completely unrestrained. If on any given day, all the police were removed from South Central, and their absence was publicized on television, it would surprise no one if looting and a riot resulted.

World Impact missionaries could have predicted the riots. We knew about the depth of hopelessness (the cause). Anything short of a riot (the symptom) should have surprised us.

What causes people to feel they have nothing to lose? What motivates customers to burn down their *own* grocery store or post office? To kill, and not care about another life, or even their own life (knowing that California has the death penalty, or life without the possibility of parole)? What drives a teenager to be willing to die for the neighborhood gang?[1] What led to the hopelessness?

---

[1] I understand martyrdom for Christianity or even Islam, but what kind of hopelessness leads a child to be willing to die for a street gang?

Once the smoke cleared it became evident that the cause of the 1992 Los Angeles riots was *BROKEN RELATIONSHIPS:* alienation between God and people, between individuals and between groups of people. Hopelessness is the personal and social evidence of alienation. This section examines the four factors that contributed to the hopelessness of 1992:

Chapter IV: Racial And Cultural Alienation
Chapter V: Class Alienation
Chapter VI: Alienation Of Families
Chapter VII: Alienation From God

The history of race relations in America, the division between the haves and have nots, the broken family and the culpability of the American Church in general are all worthy of our attention because they are within our power, through God, to change.

Chapter IV

Racial and Cultural Alienation[1]

Racial and cultural alienation were the most obvious contributors to the hopelessness that caused the 1992 riots. A Black man was beaten by White police. An African-American child was killed by a Korean-American grocer. Race and culture were immediately tagged as the culprits. Racial prejudice and cultural conflict have plagued America since the first Europeans stepped on our shores.

An Historical Perspective on Race Relations in America

This section is not a definitive study of race relations in America—a complex, painful and troublesome topic that would take volumes to explore. Instead, I attempt to set a context for the pain and anger generated daily over racial bitterness and hatred. The conflict among races in our country started over 400 years ago, before our nation's birth. As a Christian I must try to understand how the history of racial mistreatment, and its memory, contributed to the Los Angeles riots and to ongoing racial animosity in America.

---

[1] The first source of broken relationships that led to alienation was conflict between races and cultures.

In The Beginning

America's history sheds light on racial and cultural relations today. When the original 13 English colonies won their independence from Britain, over 77% of the population spoke English, which was adopted as the common language. Non-English colonials were regarded as aliens and were obliged to adapt to the English rule of law, politics and culture.

Our founding fathers, including Benjamin Franklin, Thomas Jefferson, George Washington and Alexander Hamilton, warned against the dangers that foreigners (any non-English speakers) would pose for the new republic.[2] The First United States Congress enacted America's initial Naturalization law, intending the United States to be a nation for "Whites only."[3]

Against this highly-prized, homogeneous backdrop, ethnic pluralism in America has its origins. How, then, did a White, Anglo-Saxon, Protestant nation become so heterogeneous? Cultural diversity was initially the result of:

- **Conquest.** Native Americans were uprooted, decimated and banished to reservations; Mexicans were conquered and annexed;
- **Slavery.** Africans were forced into perpetual servanthood; and
- **Exploitation of foreign labor.** Immigrants were imported to provide labor for industrial development.[4]

Three different perspectives on life in the United States have emerged out of the various ways in which America became culturally diverse: the view of those in the dominant culture; the view of those from integrated cultures (who came voluntarily); and the view of those from oppressed cultures (who were forced to become part of the United States).[5]

---

[2] Stephen Steinberg, *The Ethnic Myth: Race, Ethnicity and Class in America,* (Boston: Beacon Press, 1981), 11-12.

[3] Claud Anderson, *Black Labor White Wealth* (Edgewood, Md.: Duncan & Duncan, 1994), 33.

[4] Steinberg, 5.

[5] Scores of people groups could have illustrated immigration experiences. The use of these few examples does not diminish the relevance of other groups.

1. **THE DOMINANT CULTURE** (White, Anglo-Saxon, Protestant) sees America as a grand experiment, a city on a hill, where all people are created equal and no matter what your past, you can achieve the American dream.

People from America's dominant culture have a difficult time grasping why all other cultures in our society do not joyfully conform to the "good life," and do not immediately respect, cherish and buy into the tremendous opportunities that America affords.

Dominant-culture citizens are fond of showcasing people from other cultures, races or classes who have "pulled themselves up by their bootstraps" and achieved the "American dream." This partly infers that an "outsider" has become acceptable to, or like, the dominant culture.

The implication is, "If *one* of them can make it, why can't they *all* succeed?" The very question widens the division and impedes communication. It assumes that the dominant culture is the standard for good, morality and success, and that all the other cultures should naturally strive to conform. This misunderstanding occurs because citizens in America's dominant culture have largely lived in racial isolation for decades, and have seldom truly communicated with other cultures and heard their perspective.

2. Those in **INTEGRATED CULTURES** chose to come to America. They see the dominant culture's description of the American dream as true, but the path to achieving it as hard. Many immigrants lost their health, wealth, dignity or lives. They were discriminated against because of appearing, acting or speaking differently. But millions overcame the odds and are proud to be Americans. Two examples of cultures that fought hard to integrate are the Chinese and the Irish.[6]

---

[6]   The examples are intended to briefly sketch the history of representative ethnicities. They are not historically exhaustive, nor inclusive of all integrating cultures.

The Chinese

By 1870, nearly 63,000 hard-working Chinese had immigrated to California, providing cheap labor. They laid the Central Pacific Railroad tracks through California and across the Sierra mountains into Utah.

The Chinese, non-White and primarily non-Christian, were considered incapable of being assimilated culturally or biologically into American society. So they suffered discrimination and harassment. Their long pigtails were cut off (which meant they could not return to China). They were beaten, mocked and victimized by random violence. For example, "in Los Angeles in 1871 a mob of Whites shot, hung and otherwise killed 20 Chinese in one night."[7]

An 1854 law prevented Chinese from testifying in court against White men, in effect declaring open season on the Chinese, who had no legal recourse when robbed, vandalized or assaulted.[8]

The Chinese Exclusion Act of 1882 drastically curtailed immigration and prevented Chinese already here from becoming naturalized American citizens. Since early Chinese immigration was predominantly male, hope of a normal family life was destroyed for most Chinese. Many men had wives and children in China whom they would not see for decades, if ever. The 1882 Act also made citizenship a prerequisite for entering many occupations or owning land. The severe economic restrictions meant that few could afford to return to China.[9]

Prejudice against the Chinese drove them into ghettos—known as Chinatowns. Few received federal unemployment relief during the Great Depression, depending instead on other Chinese for support and rehabilitation. In 1900 the proportion of Chinese in the professions was lower than that of Blacks; the percentage of Asian domestic servants was twice as high as Blacks. In 1860, the California Superintendent of Education

[7] Thomas Sowell, *Ethnic America*, (New York: Basic Books, 1981), 137.

[8] Roger Daniels and Harry Kitano, *American Racism* (Englewood Cliffs, N.J.: Prentice-Hall, 1970).

[9] Sowell, 5.

defined Chinese as an "inferior race" and barred Asians from attending the same schools as Whites.[10]

In contrast, Chinese Americans today have higher incomes and higher occupational status than Americans in general. One fourth of all employed Chinese Americans work in scientific and professional fields. In the midst of great opposition, the Chinese achieved the American dream.

The Irish

The Irish were the first major ethnic minority in American cities. Fleeing the potato famine in Ireland, they arrived in the 1820's at the bottom of the urban occupational ladder as manual laborers or maids. They crowded into dilapidated housing and lived under disease-ridden conditions. They were frequent victims of fire, violence, alcoholism and crime.

"No Irish need apply" was a common posting for sought-after jobs during that time. Because of this, the Irish did menial, dirty and dangerous work: they built the infrastructure of our nation—railroads, canals and coal mines.

In the 1840's, most homeless orphans were assumed to be Irish: their economic condition in the 19th century was the worst of any racial or ethnic group in American history. They died younger and lived in poorer housing than most southern slaves. In 1914, half the Irish families on Manhattan's West side were fatherless.

The nickname, "The Fighting Irish," referred to individual brawls and mass melees (donnybrooks) for which the Irish were known. Paradoxically, these notorious fighters and drinkers built churches and schools wherever they went in America.

Because the Irish spoke English and became politically organized, they rose out of poverty to surpass the American average of income and education. The Irish are now so Americanized that some lament that they have lost their distinctive qualities,

---

[10] Robert Lee, *Guide to Chinese American Philanthropy & Charitable Giving Patterns* (San Rafael, CA: Pitney Press, 1990), 10.

while others point out that assimilating as Americans was their dream.[11]

3. Unlike those from the dominant culture and from integrated cultures, people from OPPRESSED CULTURES did not choose to become Americans. They were forcibly removed from their homelands and in the process were raped, murdered, dehumanized, oppressed and exploited. Today, many have assimilated into middle-class America; some even work toward reconciliation with different cultures and races. But the majority still feel oppressed and many remain angry and resentful.

Native Americans

The White man disregarded the humanity of Native Americans. Columbus abducted six Indians in full regalia and decorated them with war paint to display to Queen Isabella. Four centuries later, when the Native Americans had been conquered, Buffalo Bill took his Wild West Show to Europe, complete with stone-faced Indians in headdress.

In between these two humiliations, the doctrine of Manifest Destiny, the belief that America should own the entire North American continent, led to the capture of Indian land and the violent elimination of the Indians who lived on the land. When Columbus "discovered" America there were 12 million Indians in North America. By the turn of the 20th Century, only 200,000 remained. Between 1850 and 1890 Native Americans were nearly exterminated.[12]

The Europeans, who came to conquer the New World, said that Indians were semi-human, blood-thirsty savages of the devil; they saw them as treacherous, barbaric and a menace to White society. In reality, many Native Americans were friendly until forced to fight back against the European policy of genocide.

The English used Genesis 3:19 to rationalize Indian genocide: "By the sweat of your brow you will eat your food." The

11 Sowell, 17ff.
12 Steinberg, 13.

soil of the earth was to be cultivated (Genesis 1:28; 9:1). The English said that Indians were blasphemously misusing the soil, because they were hunters, not farmers (many Native Americans were agrarian, but were killed anyway).

Theodore Roosevelt wrote in *The Winning of the West*, "The settler and pioneer have at bottom had justice on their side; this great continent could not have been kept as nothing but a game preserve for squalid savages."[13]

In 1838, 20,000 Cherokee were rounded up at bayonet-point and interned in stockades, where 2500 died. In the winter of that year, 4000 more Native Americans died in a grueling, forced march to Kansas, causing the Cherokee to call it, "The Trail of Tears."[14]

The 1861 Treaty of Fort Wise gave Native Americans Sand Creek, a small amount of useless land in Colorado. But they resented the deal, and left the reservation to attack and kill Whites.[15]

Then in November, 1864, the southern Cheyenne and Arapaho wanted peace, surrendered at Fort Lyon and returned to the Sand Creek Reservation. There, Colonel John Chimington, a Methodist preacher, massacred 105 women and children and 28 men who were living peacefully on the reservation. Most of the young men were away hunting for food.[16]

Rev. Chimington justified his actions: "I have come to kill Indians. I believe it is right and honorable to use any means under God's heaven to kill Indians."[17] Chimington's army scalped and mutilated the Indians, dismembered their fingers to get rings and cut off women's bosoms and wore them on their heads. His troops were hailed as conquering heroes.

[13] Wilkomb E. Wasburn, "The Moral and Legal Justifications for Dispossessing the Indians" *17th Century America*, James Morton Smith, ed., (Chapel Hill: University of North Carolina Press, 1959), 23.

[14] "Cherokee" *Funk and Wagnalls Encyclopedia*. (Infopedia 2.0 computer software, SoftKey International: 1995).

[15] Dee Brown, *Bury My Heart At Wounded Knee*, (New York: Simon & Shuster, 1970), 69.

[16] Brown, 86.

[17] Brown, 85.

By 1888, the United States government broke the resistance of the Native Americans and forced them onto reservations. The Indian barrier to Manifest Destiny was destroyed. Two cultures were contending for a continent. One "won," and one lost.

During the 100 years since Native Americans were driven onto reservations, few have recovered from the theft of their land and dignity. Many have succumbed to alcoholism, substance abuse, broken homes and welfare dependency. Some have assimilated into society, experiencing economic resurgence through lucrative resorts, gambling operations, mining concessions and Native-American art. Despite strong resistance to the White man's gospel, there are signs of openness to Christ.[18]

Mexican Americans

The war against Mexico culminated with the 1848 Treaty of Guadalupe-Hidalgo, which transferred one-third of Mexico's land (now the American Southwest) to the United States. The treaty preserved the land holdings of Mexicans living in this region and their right to use Spanish as their primary language.[19]

However, laws began to exclude Mexican Americans from voting and applying for citizenship, because they were considered "Indians," who were restricted from having these rights.[20] Within a decade most Mexican Americans had lost their land because of illegal land-grant dealings by Anglos.[21] Mexican Americans were stereotyped as an evil, inferior race,[22] consid-

---

[18] Lee Grady, "America's Forgotten People" *Charisma*, October 1994 (Vol 20, No 3), 24-30.

[19] Ramon A. Gutierrez, "Historical and social science research on Mexican Americans," in *Handbook of research on multicultural education*, ed. James A. Banks and Cherry A. McGee Banks (New York: Macmillan, 1995), 206.

[20] Robert F. Heizer and Alan F. Almquist, *The Other Californians: Prejudice and Discrimination Under Spain, Mexico, and the United States to 1920* (Berkeley, CA.: University of California Press, 1971), 60, 62, 150-151.

[21] Albert Camarillo, *Chicanos in California: A History of Mexican Americans in California* (San Francisco: Boyd & Fraser Publishing Company, 1984), 14-15.

[22] Martha Menchaca and Richard R. Valencia, "Anglo-Saxon ideologies in the 1920's-1930's: Their impact on the segregation of Mexican students in California," *Anthropology & Education Quarterly* 21, no. 3 (1990): 222-249.

ered simple-minded, indolent and savage.[23]

By the middle of the 19th century, race crimes were common.[24] An 1857 California law barred Mexican Americans from testifying in court against Anglos.[25] Residential segregation was enforced through racial harassment, violence and housing-covenant restrictions.[26] If Mexican-American children attended school, they were segregated from White children in overcrowded schools which had inexperienced teachers and few supplies.[27]

Later immigrants from Mexico were barred from community swimming pools, theaters, businesses, restaurants and housing.[28] During World War II, signs around Los Angeles establishments proclaimed, "Tuesdays reserved for Negroes and Mexicans."[29]

By the mid-1980's, Hispanics had completed fewer grades of school and had higher dropout rates than Whites or African Americans (Mexican Americans represent over 60% of Hispanics in the United States, and over 80% of Hispanics in California and Texas). Today, almost one third of the Hispanics in the United States live in poverty.[30]

In spite of incredible barriers, Mexican Americans have contributed food, sports, music and festivals to the North American culture. They are increasingly entering universities,

---

[23] David Weber, *The Mexican Frontier, 1821-1846: The American Southwest Under Mexico* (Albuquerque: University of New Mexico Press, 1982), xvi.

[24] Albert Camarillo, *Chicanos in a Changing Society: From Mexican Pueblos to American Barrios in Santa Barbara and Southern California, 1848-1930* (Cambridge, MA: Harvard University Press, 1979), 18.

[25] Menchaca and Valencia, 229.

[26] Ruben Donato, Martha Menchaca, and Richard R. Valencia, "Segregation, Desegregation, and Integration of Chicago Students: Problems and Prospects," in *Chicago School Failure and Success: Research and Policy Agendas for the 1990's,* ed. Richard R. Valencia (New York: Falmer Press, 1991), 34.

[27] Irving G. Hendrick, *The Education of Non-Whites in California, 1849-1970,* (San Francisco: R. E. Research Associates, Inc., 1977), 7; Meyer Weinberg, *A Chance to Learn: The History of Race and Education in the United States* (New York: Cambridge University Press, 1977), 140-145; David Montejano, *Anglos and Mexicans in the Making of Texas, 1836-1986* (Austin: University of Texas Press, 1987), 192.

[28] Camarillo, 39, 41, 70, 79, 83; Hendrick, 99.

[29] Camarillo, 39, 41.

[30] Patricia Gandara, *Over the Ivy Walls: The Educational Mobility of Low-Income Chicanos* (Albany, NY: State University of New York Press, 1995), 2.

professions and government positions. And the gospel is spreading rapidly among them.

African Americans

The first Negroes brought to Virginia in 1619 were indentured servants. At the end of their servitude, they could become free. While both Whites and Blacks were indentured servants, Whites came to America voluntarily; Blacks were brought by force.[31] And there was another difference: in 1638, Negro servanthood became permanent.[32]

Racial Prejudice

The English treated White servants differently from Negroes because Whites considered the Negro innately inferior.[33] There were at least five reasons for this prejudice.

1. When the English came into contact with Negroes in the mid-1500's, the English viewed the color black as a stigma connoting gloom, filth, dirt, misfortune, wretchedness, the devil or harm. Shakespeare had used black as a sign of danger or corruption, as in MacBeth's witches or Othello. Milton equated darkness with evil or death. God brought light into darkness; black was the color of hell. In contrast, the color white symbolized goodness, cleanliness, virginity, innocence, purity and virtue.

2. The English interpreted the Bible to support their views on Africans and slavery. Africans were considered pagans and heathens; their dark skin was attributed to Noah's curse of Ham. This image of Africans as savages conjured up visions of naked tribesmen decapitating foes, drinking human blood and worshiping snakes in the depths of a jungle. Africa was called the

---

[31] Lerone Bennett, Jr., *Before the Mayflower: A History of Black America,* (New York: Penguin Books, 1982), 47.

[32] Winthrop D. Jordan, *White Over Black: American Attitudes Toward the Negro, 1550-1812,* (Baltimore: Penguin Books, 1969), 66.

[33] C. Vann Woodward, *The Strange Career of Jim Crow,* (London, New York: Oxford University Press, 1966), 11.

dark continent.[34] Slave owners noted the existence of slavery in the Old Testament; Jesus recognized slavery and did not explicitly abolish it; Paul told slaves to obey their masters.

3. Many Whites viewed the Negro as a beast without a rational soul. In the 1690's, several educated Europeans believed that Negroes had apes for ancestors, partly because their coloring was similar to that of apes.[35]

4. The English viewed the Negro as criminal and lazy, innately predisposed to treachery and theft. In 1713, the New Jersey legislature limited freeing slaves because free Negroes were "idle and slothful."[36]

5. Many English believed that Negroes were less intelligent than Whites. Voltaire said Negroes were incapable of abstract thinking. Thomas Jefferson noted that Negroes could not reflect. Edmund Ruffin thought they were intellectually inferior; several abolitionists agreed.[37]

From Prejudice to Slavery

Racial prejudice was the major contributor to slavery, which was the institutionalization of racism. White masters owned Black slaves. Racial prejudice and slavery reinforced each other. To be Black was to be property, contemptible and oppressed.

In the 1660's, Virginia and Maryland legalized slavery, making Blacks slaves for life.[38] By 1700, slavery was established in every colony. All servants imported from non-Christian countries were slaves for life, even if they converted to Christianity. Children born to an enslaved woman, even by a White father, were considered slaves. Therefore, slave status became self-perpetuating and hereditary.[39]

---

[34] Many Africans lived in settlements, raised crops and cattle, and were highly-skilled craftsmen (in iron and gold) who maintained political and family institutions. Slave traders did business with several African governments on equal terms.

[35] Jordan, 228.

[36] Jordan, 124.

[37] Avery O'Craven, _Edmund Ruffin: Southerner,_ (Baton Rouge: LSU Press, 1966), 173.

[38] Daniel P. Mannix, _Black Cargoes,_ (New York: Viking Press, 1962), 60.

[39] George M. Stroud, _A Sketch of the Laws Relating to Slavery in The Several States of the United States of America,_ 2nd ed. (Philadelphia: H. Longstreth, 1856), 60-61.

Property, Not People

America became a contradiction. The land Europeans pictured as a Garden of Eden (pure, virgin and innocent) with the lure of equality and freedom, enslaved ten million Africans between 1500 and 1800. Most of the framers of our Declaration of Independence and Constitution, and even John Locke, who wrote the "Natural Rights Philosophy," owned slaves. Patrick Henry ("Give me liberty or give me death") did not liberate his slaves.

How could slaves, who had no rights, exist in America, which claimed to believe that all men are created equal, with the right to life, liberty and the pursuit of happiness? Our founding fathers' answer to this dilemma was to declare that slaves were property, not people.

A 1669 Virginia law defined slaves as property. It was not a felony for a master to employ corporal punishment to correct a slave. The 1680 "Black codes" restricted Blacks' freedom of movement and their personal rights, and regulated their conduct. South Carolina designated slaves as real estate in 1690. By 1740, slaves were defined as movable property.[40]

Since slaves were considered property, they could not make legal contracts; contracts required personhood and free moral agency. Negroes could not testify in a White trial, since that implied moral intelligence.[41]

Because slaves could not legally enter into a marriage contract, fathers had no legal relationship to their children, and wives or children could be sold away from their families. There was no legal infidelity or adultery. Therefore, male slaves had no recourse against another man for having intercourse with his wife. As a result, the female was reduced to a breeding animal.[42]

Because property cannot own property, it was illegal for slaves to own dogs.[43] South Carolina prohibited teaching slaves to read

[40] Frank Tannenbaum, *Slave and Citizen* (New York: Random House, 1946), 72.
[41] Jordan, 407.
[42] Tannenbaum, 81.
[43] Tannenbaum, 76-77.

or write because property (i.e., a book) can be read, but cannot read or write. Being unable to read maps or signs made control easier and impeded escape, since safe houses or the Underground Railroad were hard for illiterates to find.

Why Not Rebellion?

Why did Africans put up with slavery? Why did they acquiesce to this bondage?

The brutal process of being enslaved destroyed their will to resist.

Of the 15 million Africans who were captured, one third died of murder, exhaustion or starvation on the forced march through Africa; or of suicide or starvation while attempting escape at the trading station on the African coast. Another third died at sea during the grueling two-month voyage to America.[44] The staggering psychological shock of enslavement[45] came in five consecutive stages.[46]

1. *The shock of capture.* Most slaves were captured in tribal wars or kidnapped in the middle of the night by mercenary fellow-Africans, who wanted to trade human beings for iron bars, beads or cloth with the Europeans.[47] The real shock came when *you* were captured and realized you were no longer free.

2. *The shock of the long and dangerous march to the sea.* Under the glaring sun, through the steaming jungle, slaves were driven like beasts tied together by their necks. Day after day, eight hours or more at a time, they staggered barefoot over thorny underbrush, dried reeds and stones. The exhausted men and women who reached the coast had experienced excruciating thirst, brutalities and near-starvation. Hundreds of bleached skeletons were strewn along the slave caravan routes.[48]

3. *The shock of being sold to the European slavers.* After the slaves were crowded into pens near the trading stations, where they

---

[44] Melville J. Herskovitz, *The Myth of The Negro Past* (Boston: Beacon, 1990).

[45] See descriptions in Henry Louis Gates, ed. *The Classic Slave Narratives* (New York: Penguin, 1987).

[46] Stanley Elkins, *Slavery* (New York: Grosset & Dunlap, 1963).

[47] Tannenbaum, 21.

[48] Elkins, 99.

sometimes stayed for days, surgeons thoroughly examined every part of their naked bodies, both men and women, without the least distinction or modesty. If bought, the slaves were branded, given numbers and herded onto ships.[49]

Those rejected were above 53 years old, lame, maimed in the arms, legs, hands or feet, or had lost a tooth. They were passed over if they had gray hair (the traders shaved every hair from a slave's body so no grey hair could be detected),[50] had film over their eyes, or had venereal distemper or other diseases. Slaves not chosen were abandoned to starvation.

4. *The shock of the Middle Passage.* Disease, death and cruelty characterized this terrible voyage. The holds, packed with squirming, suffocating humanity, became stinking infernos of filth. Slaves were allowed a space barely larger than a grave —5 feet 6 inches long by 16 inches broad, and 2 to 3 feet high—not high enough to sit up.[51] There was little ventilation. For 15 or 16 hours a day slaves were kept below deck in the stench—dark, steamy, slimy and wet—without sanitation or running water. They were naked and chained to one another at the ankles. The skin over their elbows was worn away from sleeping without covering on unplaned boards on a stormy passage.[52]

Rebellion or mutiny was punished swiftly—hanging from the mast or walking the plank.[53] When ships ran out of water, captains threw some slaves overboard to save the rest. Many slaves went mad and tried to commit suicide by jumping overboard.[54] Slaves who tried to starve themselves to death were forced to swallow hot coals—a warning that deterred others.[55]

5. *The shock of being resold.* When the Negroes arrived in the West Indies (the gateway to America) the boat fired a gun and a crowd of buyers would run aboard the ships. Potential cus-

[49] Elkins, 99.
[50] Mannix, 46.
[51] Tannenbaum, 23.
[52] Mannix, 104-105.
[53] Tannenbaum, 26.
[54] Mannix, 113.
[55] Mannix, 119.

tomers manhandled the slaves, who were lined up naked in public for inspection. Some Negroes jumped overboard in sheer fright.

The Negroes were examined, felt, measured and haggled over like cattle, reminiscent of their treatment in the African markets. The buyer would mark his prize with a sign, decorate his acquisition with a hat and a handkerchief and march him off to be branded.[56]

Not only were the slaves' will to resist destroyed, their past was annihilated as well.

Every prior connection was severed. Slaves had no hope of regaining their family, language or tribal religion. Old values were destroyed. Slaves were coerced into polygamy and forced sex with their masters. Slave breeding decimated the family unit. Slave women were workers first, so the older children took care of the younger ones.

Everything depended on the will of the slave's new master: food, clothes, life, shelter, sexual connections, whatever moral instruction might be offered, whatever "success" was possible within the system.[57]

Masters prevented escape by keeping slaves dependent, ignorant and in fear. Frederick Law Olmsted concluded that the southern strategy was to train slaves to work, yet prevent them from learning to take care of themselves.[58] It took slaves generations to recover from this systemic dehumanization.

Emancipation

By 1776, the dominant culture generally acknowledged slavery as a national moral wrong,[59] and the economics no longer demanded slave labor, but racial prejudice remained. Slavery was a social system as much as a labor system.[60]

Even after the Emancipation Proclamation of 1863, to kill a Negro was not deemed murder; to rape a Negro was not a crime;

---

[56] Elkins, 100.
[57] Elkins, 102.
[58] Lenone Bennett Jr., 109.
[59] Jordan, 279.
[60] Sowell, 194.

to steal from a Negro was not robbery. Blacks had no rights which White people were bound by law to respect. This led to Ku Klux Klan terrorism, lynchings and mob violence.

Jim Crow laws codified the divisions between the races.[61] Water fountains, railroad cars, boats and prostitutes were segregated. Social rituals developed which maintained polite distance and deference to Whites. Negroes dared not look a White person in the eye. Both races accommodated this unequal social contract which required Negroes to stay in their place.

Migration to cities like New York, Detroit, Chicago and Los Angeles helped change the segregated status of African Americans. The cities furnished employment and education opportunities lacking in the rural South.

Then the Civil Rights Movement, begun in the 1950's, sparked a breakthrough for African Americans. Many advanced to prominent positions in government, business, sports and entertainment. In contrast, most inner-city Blacks remained trapped in welfare, single-parent families, teenage pregnancy, unemployment, drug addiction and crime.

Black leaders now call for a return to the Church and the moral identity that sustained the African-American family and community through long years of persecution and rejection by society.[62] Such restored moral identity offers hope for the future.

DIFFERING PERSPECTIVES

The foregoing historical examples help us understand how a person's view of America is substantially influenced by how one got here—by choice or by force—and how well one has integrated into the dominant culture. Immigrants *choosing* to come to the United States have historically integrated faster and fared better than those *forced* to become Americans.

In an effort to populate our large land mass, build our infrastructure, work our mills and factories, and pick our cotton, a

---

[61] Woodward, 11.

[62] Alan Keyes, *Masters of the Dream: The Strength and Betrayal of Black America*, (New York: William Morrow, 1995), 58.

country that prided itself on its ethnic homogeneity became the most polyglot nation in history.[63] Lady Liberty welcomed some immigrants with open arms; others in chains.[64]

Since the dominant culture ignored oppressed cultures, communication diminished and understanding faded. The dominant culture has been racially prejudiced against those who are different. The greater the racial difference, the greater the prejudice.

For example, it seemed "apparent" to "reasonable Americans" after Pearl Harbor that we should distrust all Japanese, even though many had been born here and raised their children here. Because they looked like the Emperor, they were suspect and subject to isolation for the good of the democracy.

One wonders why German Americans were not thrown into detention camps, since they could have been mistaken for the Führer. Perhaps being a first cousin to the dominant culture warranted an exception.

I must include one observation after this rehearsal of America's less than honorable multi-cultural origins. In spite of slavery, racism, discrimination and prejudice, the United States is the most attractive destination on earth for immigrants. It is still the land of social, economic and political opportunity. Millions continue to risk their lives to come here. There are no walls to prevent the departure of dissatisfied residents.

Reviewing our nation's struggles neither belittles our greatness nor ignores God's obvious blessings upon us. Patriotism does not deny our history nor cover our blemishes. Instead, it seeks the truth, which sets people free, and helps us avoid repeating past sins.

Reflecting on our treatment of fellow citizens heightens our understanding of why certain segments of society view things so differently. Hopefully all citizens will seek reconciliation with hurt or offended brothers and sisters, which will promote a more perfect union.

---

[63] Steinberg, 301.
[64] Of course, most slaves did not sail into New York Harbor, or pass by The Statue of Liberty which was donated by France to America in 1866.

Race Relations In 1992

While much of our treatment of immigrants has not been admirable, most Americans in the dominant culture and many from the integrating cultures, have come to view the United States as a melting pot—where immigrants ceased to be Irish, African, Chinese or Mexican and became Americans. *I want to be an American* was the cry of new immigrants.

During the Eisenhower years, the dominant culture began to believe that we had learned to get along with each other, almost prophetically setting the stage for "Camelot." But then the Civil Rights Movement spurred racial and cultural pride, and America's long-revered melting pot was replaced by a multi-cultural boiling pot.

By 1992, 106 languages were spoken in Los Angeles public schools—representing over 157 major people groups. And we did not get along with each other.[65]

A diverse population was not new to America. We are a nation of immigrants. So what was unique in 1992 that led to such intense turmoil?

Massive New Immigration

Since 1989, Southern California has been America's leading center for new immigrants (primarily from Latin America and Asia), welcoming more than twice as many as second-place New York.[66] The internationalization of Los Angeles' inner city through large-scale immigration had several results.

First, it impeded assimilation. Vast numbers of new immigrants arrived simultaneously from such diverse backgrounds that many did not bother to learn how to relate to people who

---

[65] More than 354 schools in Los Angeles County reported incidents of hate crimes against students or employees in a one-year period. Anti-immigrant hate crimes (471) were perpetrated primarily against Latinos and Asian-Pacific Americans. "Race, Power and Promise in Los Angeles: An Assessment of Responses to Human Relations Conflict," *The Multi-Cultural Collaborative* (Los Angeles: Jan., 1996) 3.

[66] Joel Kotkin, "Los Angeles' Engine of Growth," *City Journal,* Winter, 1993: 61.

were different. As a result, thousands of Hispanic and Asian immigrants never tried to assimilate into a new culture or community. A Korean could live, work, shop, worship, practice his lifelong customs and conduct all his business in Korean. For all intents and purposes, he might as well be living in Pusan or Seoul. The same was true for a Guatemalan, Mexican or Nicaraguan. The lack of a common language polarized the unassimilated. Such large-scale separatism was new to America.

Second, the ethnic, cultural and racial tolerance of existing Americans was stretched to the breaking point. Fewer jobs created intense competition. The unemployed were agitated by immigrants "taking our jobs." As a result, people of different cultures, or different classes within the same ethnicity, lived in conflict.

For example, two-thirds of the mothers giving birth at Los Angeles County Hospital in 1990-1991 were immigrants who had entered the country illegally.[67] Tired of paying for undocumented immigrants, some Latinos threatened to leave the State Democratic Party unless it supported bills against illegal immigrants.[68] This tension arose between different classes within the same ethnicity.

Finally, many immigrants brought racism and prejudices with them that they maintained here. For example, Mexicans and Salvadorans have long been rivals and remain so in the United States. Similarly, Central Americans have imported their "pecking order" of status, based on nationality, which has resulted in more friction here.

Old Domestic Divisions

In 1992, Martin Luther King's dream of a color-blind integrated society, once thought to be universally accepted, was being challenged by separatism. Many groups declared their

---

[67] There are between four and six million undocumented aliens nationally—half are in California, which claims the 1994-1995 cost of services to illegal immigrants will be equivalent to 750,000 tax-paying jobs.

[68] Charles Mahtesian, "Immigration: The Symbolic Crackdown," *Governing Magazine*, May, 1994: 52-54.

rights, and few counted others as better than, or even equal to, themselves.[69]

Separatism defies our national motto, *E Pluribus Unum:* out of many, one. Originally referring to 13 colonies becoming one nation, the motto encourages every ethnic group to become one (Americans) when they enter this inclusive nation.

While understanding and valuing a person's or group's national heritage is crucial, multiculturalism is dangerous if it undermines the inclusiveness ensured by the Constitution; or if it denigrates Western culture, which introduced individual freedom, tolerance, political democracy and human rights; or if it turns America into a nation of groups instead of a nation of individuals. Thomas Sowell, a Black economist at Stanford, warns, "You want to see multiculturalism in action? Look at Yugoslavia, at Lebanon, at Sri Lanka, at Northern Ireland, Azerbaijan, or wherever else group identity has been hyped."[70]

Racism is not unique to White Americans. It is a human sin problem manifested in Rwanda, Bosnia and the Middle East. Every dominant culture views itself as the best. Ethnocentrism is a sociological certainty. America did not escape its influence. Tragically, the objects of racism frequently become racists themselves, trapping both the culprit and the victim in bitter, diabolical hatred that displeases God.

Racial and cultural conflict were the most obvious factors that led to the hopelessness that caused the 1992 riots. But they were not the only factors.

---

[69] "Racial polarization and ethnic conflict in Los Angeles were reaching alarming dimensions. Interracial violence in Los Angeles public schools and neighborhoods was growing. Anti-immigrant sentiment in local communities and institutions was rising. The criminalization of masses of African-American and Latino young men had grown appallingly acceptable. And the backdrop to these realities was the widening economic divide between the city's haves and have nots." *The Multi-Cultural Collaborative,* 3.

[70] Dan Quayle, "Multiculturalism: Sounds Nice, But It Has Dangers," *USA Today,* 7 Dec., 1995: 11A.

Chapter V

Class Alienation[1]

While racial and cultural conflict was the most obvious source of alienation, class polarization also contributed to the hopelessness that spawned the 1992 riots.

Economic Separation

An increasing chasm had developed between the haves and the have nots. The rich became richer, the poor became poorer, and especially in the inner cities, fewer in-betweens existed.

Real wages had dropped, particularly among poor Blacks and Hispanics.[2] The cost of durable goods (cars, housing) and higher education had increased. Rampant divorce reduced spendable income for families by creating two households—one of which was often a single mother with inadequate child support. Meanwhile, the expectations of the poor were heightened by seductive advertisement and peer pressure.

Unemployment increased as industries relocated out of the city to avoid violence, congestion, pollution and the high cost of labor and taxes. Inner-city men had difficulty supporting their families financially. The street-corner drug trade became the

---

[1] The second source of broken relations that led to alienation was enmity between classes.

[2] Lynn A. Karoly, "The Widening Income and Wage Gap Between Rich and Poor," *Urban America: Policy Choices for Los Angeles and The Nation* (Santa Monica: Rand, 1992) 55-81.

major employer of the young.[3]

Physical Isolation

The poor and the affluent had little personal knowledge of one another in spite of television's in-depth coverage of both. Their worlds were as different as night and day.

Sometimes I transported the rich to the poor, and other times the poor to the rich. Their reactions were predictable: "I had no idea the other class existed like this."

Frequently this trans-class journey produced envy or resentment; or it led to pity or fear. Unless viewed through Christ's compassionate perspective, and immersed in good communication, exposure often stimulated wider divisions and sickening prejudices.

People from both classes commonly made dehumanizing, stereotypical generalizations about each other. This resulted in irrational justifications on both sides.[4] Some rich demanded long prison terms for the poor; some poor defended stealing from the prosperous.[5] And the gulf between the haves and have nots expanded.

At the outbreak of the riots many urban residents lived in abject poverty.[6] Numerous children lacked adequate food, clothing, shoes or shelter. So when an immoral opportunity disguised itself as a free shopping spree, self-appointed philosophers announced, "These stores have ripped us off for generations. Take whatever you want. The merchant owes it to us." Just as in ancient Israel, "Everyone did what was right in his own eyes" (Judges 21:25, NASB).

---

[3]   Deborah Prothrow-Stith, M.D., *Deadly Consequences*, (New York: Harper Perennial, 1991), 115.

[4]   See Nicholas Lemann, "The Origins of the Underclass," *The Atlantic Monthly*, June and July, 1986, for an explanation of how "haves" and "have nots" are growing within the same racial groups.

[5]   Greg Krikorian, "Study Questions Justice System's Racial Fairness," *Los Angeles Times*, 13 Feb., 1996: A17.

[6]   In 1991, the median household net worth for non-Anglos was $1,353 compared to $31,904 for Anglos. *Inside The Los Angeles Riots*, (Institute of Alternative Journalism, 1992), 32.

Emotions won the day. Many people succumbed to the temptation to steal. Thieves drove pickup trucks to stores and brazenly removed all the merchandise they could transport. Some audacious criminals hired a taxi and went to a Fedco Department Store, commanded the cab to wait, stole everything they could from the retailer, loaded their booty into the cab and instructed the driver to take them home—in spite of cameras documenting their actions on national television.

Other looters, with merchandise in hand, stopped to be interviewed by television reporters, perversely justifying their theft by declaring, "I deserve it." Morality, the basic understanding of what is right and wrong, was sorely missing.

Isaiah 59:14-15 came to life that day on the streets of Los Angeles: "So justice is driven back, and righteousness stands at a distance; truth has stumbled in the streets, honesty cannot enter. Truth is nowhere to be found, and whoever shuns evil becomes a prey. The Lord looked and was displeased that there was no justice."

Several merchants, realizing that they were on their own, "gave" away all of their goods in exchange for the looters agreeing not to torch their buildings. Others posted "Black Owned" signs on their doors hoping they would be spared, thinking maybe the rioters only wanted to lash out against perceived economic exploitation of the Black community. Sometimes it worked; more often it did not. Most such businesses learned it was hard to deal with the devil and his henchmen.

One African-American couple, who owned a tire store across the street from the Los Angeles Coliseum, watched helplessly as decades of hard work exploded in an afternoon. Years of corporate responsibility and civic pride mattered little to the greedy and lawless.

Early Friday morning, May 1, 1992, I stopped (intending to buy gas) at an Arco AM/PM Mini-Market. However, there was no attendant; no front door. A man was standing outside of the building looking at his unimpaired access to all the Cokes, beer and fast foods he ever wanted. There were no police to deter him; those items were his for the taking. I said, "Don't take them, or you will never forgive yourself."

One seldom gets something for nothing. A few residents, who had stolen furniture and appliances, put their old couches and refrigerators on the curb to be picked up by the garbage men. The police documented these actions and retrieved the stolen items, leaving the residents with neither old nor new appliances or furniture.

Some parents forced their children to help them loot: more hands meant more goods. Several Bible-club children had to disobey their parents, or steal. Other Bible-club youngsters asked if they should eat food that their relatives had looted. One elected official chanted, "No justice, no peace." She got neither.

Because they were physically isolated and did not understand each other, the have nots justified their looting by pointing to the injustice of the haves. In turn, the haves responded predictably: "Throw the book at the criminals. Put them in jail and lose the keys."

And so the poor felt alienated from the middle and upper class. The poor believed they were being exploited by absentee landlords and by businesses who did not give back to the neighborhood or relocated out of the inner city. They saw the American Dream portrayed on television but were unable to participate in it.

Government Detachment

The poor also viewed the government (police, schools, welfare, politicians) as a different class of people ruling them. Many believed that the bureaucrats, law makers and law enforcers knew little about the underclass, and cared even less. Few government employees were from the community they served.

Most of the poor mistrusted the police particularly. Not only were residents afraid they might be abused, they resented the police's inability to maintain order in the city. Many people feared they would be the next victims of violence.[7]

---

[7] Prothrow-Stith, 82.

Urban teenagers knew they lived in a dangerous place. In fact, 25,000 inner-city teenagers were murdered in America in 1993, making it more dangerous to grow up in our inner cities than it was to be an American soldier in combat in Viet Nam.[8] The homicide rate for 15-24-year-olds in America was five times higher than any other country.[9]

Since "a gang homicide costs society up to $1 million,"[10] few understood why the nation did not spend those funds to stop the murders, especially when they saw that it is possible to reduce crime dramatically. When government officials and the business community worked together to host the 1984 Olympics in the inner city of Los Angeles, it became the safest neighborhood in America! People wondered, then, if the have nots were simply not worth the effort, or the resources, of the haves.

Government inefficiency also hurt the poor. The number of managers in government had grown twice as fast as the frontline employees. For example, in 1960 there were more than two teachers for every administrator. Now there is one administrator for every teacher.[11]

Through the 1980's, state and local government employee growth outstripped population growth two to one (rising 20% in twelve years).[12]

John Chubb, a Senior Fellow at Brookings, argued that bloat was not just too many people. It was a stifling array of

---

[8] *The San Francisco Examiner,* 26 Sept., 1993: A4.

[9] *The San Francisco Examiner,* A4.

[10] "Medical Researchers Call Gang Killings 'Epidemic in County,'" *Los Angeles Times,* 4 Oct., 1995.

[11] Jonathan Walters, "The Shrink-Proof Bureaucracy," *Governing Magazine,* Mar., 1992.

[12] Washington D.C. public employment increased as their population declined. From 1980-1990, Philadelphia city employment increased by .01%, while management positions rose 15.5%. For the same period in New York, employment was up 24% with management positions increasing 50%.

New York City's Public Library system has had the same number of libraries since 1950, *but* librarians and researchers have decreased from 1700 to 1500. In contrast, top-level library management has increased from two assistant directors and a small support staff, to a president, eight vice presidents, two directors, ten associate directors and dozens of other managers. Walters, 33-38.

administrative practices from procuring to hiring to contracting to performance evaluation that lessened productivity everywhere in the system. For example, it took 90 days in Washington D.C. schools to get supplies from a central delivery office. This inefficiency hindered the education of the poor.

Seventy-five percent of government aid intended for the poor went to bureaucrats, not to the poor.[13] If World Impact spent 75% of its resources on administration I would be writing from the Los Angeles County jail. One reason many middle-class Blacks favored maintaining or even expanding government was that 70% of Black college graduates were employed by government.[14] While excessive bureaucracy helped the middle class through employment, it hurt the poor by reducing the money that could be spent on them.

This government inefficiency led to over-taxed cities losing businesses, leaving the urban poor without jobs or a tax base. Because of this, cities could not pay for adequate school teachers or policemen.

In summary, the poor felt exploited by government "which abandoned us or punished us for our poverty,"[15] and afraid of, unprotected and even abused by the police. This alienation from government, along with the estrangement caused by the physical and economic separation between the poor and the rich, contributed to the hopelessness that caused the 1992 riots.

---

[13] Robert L. Woodson "Poverty: Why Politics Can't Cure It," *The Presbyterian Layman*, Nov./Dec., 1988: 9.

[14] Claud Anderson, *Black Labor White Wealth* (Edgewood, Md.: Duncan & Duncan, 1994), 33. 190.

[15] Maxine Waters, "Testimony Before The Senate Banking Committee" *Inside The Los Angeles Riots*, 26.

Chapter VI

Alienation of Families[1]

The broken family (husbands alienated from their wives, and parents from their children) was a major contributor to the riots, and is the Achilles heel of urban society. Seventy-five percent of the children born in our inner cities are born out of wedlock. Further documenting the deteriorating status of the urban family with multiple statistics would be overkill.

But what caused the urban family to splinter?

Nicholas Lemann explains the roots of the underclass in America, the proliferation of broken families in our inner cities, by documenting two massive migrations of African Americans.[2] The first migration was geographical and formed the foundation for the second migration.

The First Migration: Out Of The South

The first migration happened during, and in between, the two World Wars, when Blacks moved from the South to the North and the West in search of jobs. During this period, all Blacks (if one-sixteenth of your blood was "Black" you were legally Black) were forced to live in the same neighborhood. "Ghetto" means "isolation."

---

[1] The third category of broken relationships that led to alienation and hopelessness was separation and divorce among family members.

[2] *Atlantic Monthly,* June, July, 1986.

As immoral as housing discrimination is, it had the unintended effect of creating a dynamic community that mixed together educated and illiterate, rich and poor, employed and unemployed, skilled and unskilled. Thus all Black children had positive African-American role models from different social classes in their neighborhood. Churches, social clubs, recreation and cultural activities flourished in their community.

For all the benefits of living in a vertically-integrated neighborhood that crossed social and class lines, being forced to live in a ghetto naturally led to feeling imprisoned. If you, your friends and family, were locked in the most wonderful room in the world, with all the amenities that made life worthwhile, but were prohibited from leaving that room, you would soon feel stifled. If, after 30 years, the door was opened, you would make a beeline for the exit.

How much more eager would you be to leave that room were it devoid of the amenities, and the stench of segregation was heavy in the air?

The Second Migration: Out Of The Ghetto

When the Civil Rights Act of 1965 made housing discrimination illegal, nearly every able-bodied Black doctor, attorney, businessman, bureaucrat, professor and educator who could do so, moved out of the inner city. This second migration, though understandable, left the inner city populated primarily by the modern-day equivalent of widows and orphans.

The children remaining in the inner city were likely to grow up in single-parent homes with few examples of two-parent families to emulate. Since we learn the most by watching and copying others, these children became single parents themselves on a radically-accelerated scale.

This process also happened among Puerto-Rican Americans, the poorest and worst-off contingent of America's underclass. Puerto-Rican communities in the inner city lost their white-collar residents at the same time the blue-collar residents lost their jobs, leading to unemployment, welfare and the family breakdown.[3]

After the second migration, many boys deprived of fathers gravitated toward the neighborhood gangs, which functioned as their surrogate family.[4] Young males in the inner city needed successful older males of color, both in and out of the inner city, to influence them to function productively within the academic, social and economic systems, and to achieve positive self images.[5]

Without responsible fathers, alcoholism and drug abuse became rampant, resulting in the physical and sexual abuse of children and spouses. Children who had been abused, frequently abused others. Youngsters who had been abandoned, ignored or oppressed had a hard time integrating into the mainstream of society. Single-parent households were more likely to function below the poverty line; poor children were less likely to graduate from high school.

However, Deborah Prothrow-Stith, former Massachusetts Commissioner of Public Health, and currently Assistant Dean of the Harvard School of Public Health explained:

"Poverty alone does not destroy a child. A poor child growing up in a stable family has a fighting chance in life. So does a child from a troubled family who grows up in a stable community. However, when schools no longer believe that children can learn, when vital city services are only meagerly apportioned, when few local businesses employ the young, when churches have less influence, or have packed up and moved to the suburbs, when few recreational facilities occupy children and when violence becomes the norm, the outlook for children is dismal. These are the circumstances of the underclass."[6]

---

[3]   Nicholas Lemann, "The Other Underclass," *Atlantic Monthly*, Dec., 1991: 96-110.
[4]   This partially answers the earlier question, "Why would a youngster die for his gang?" Because it is his family.
[5]   Ron Ferguson, "The Case For Community-Based Programs that Inform and Mentor Black Male Youth," *Urban Institute Research Paper*, Washington, D.C., n.d.
[6]   Prothrow-Stith, 75.

The child who felt he was so worthless that his father did not stay around to raise him, or was so bad that he caused his father to leave, experienced intense alienation. This affected every area of his life—education, employment, family relations and general health—all of which feed hopelessness.

Certainly, the broken family fueled the flames of alienation that fostered the 1992 riots.

Chapter VII

Alienation From God[1]

The root cause of all alienation—from God and from each other—is sin. The antidote to sin is a personal relationship with God through Christ. This leads to hope, reconciliation and healing. God usually initiates a personal relationship with an individual, and then nurtures it, through His Church.

Many of the urban poor had no personal relationship with God. Consequently, they had no body of believers to support, love, encourage and teach them. God's Word was not a light unto their paths.

The Church in Los Angeles should have been the source of healing and reconciliation for the poor. It should have been the voice crying out in the city: "Behold the Lamb of God Who takes away the sins of the world." It should have been the Shepherd searching for the lost sheep, carefully, lovingly bringing them into the fold, assuring the doubters, "Come home! Come home! You who are weary, come home."

But tragically, much of the Church was conspicuous by its absence from the urban poor. For the most part, the Church had acted as if it were unconcerned about "the least of these brothers" of Christ (Matthew 25:40).

---

[1] The fourth source of broken relationships that led to alienation was the division between man and God.

The Unchurched

Only one half of one percent of the 4.5 million Hispanics in greater Los Angeles consider themselves to be evangelical Christians. Yet almost one percent of the people in all Latin-American cities claim to be evangelical Christians. That makes Los Angeles the most unevangelized Hispanic city in the Latin world![2]

America is no longer a "Christian" nation. Less than 20% of the population meet for worship on any given Sunday.[3] In Miami only 7.9% of the population attend church (Catholic or Protestant).[4] A 1983 Gallup Poll indicated that no more than 12% of Americans are highly committed to religion.[5]

The 1980's saw the largest immigration in our nation's history. Ninety percent of the immigrants were non-European; 15% were Muslim, adding to the five million already here. One out of seven people (i.e., 32 million) in the United States speaks a language other than English at home. People from the 10/40 window[6] are *here*; hidden peoples are our neighbors, and their numbers are multiplying rapidly.

And yet, of recent immigrants, fewer than 10% will be invited into any American home, let alone a Christian home, during their *first ten years* in the United States. Believers border on hypocrisy when they pray for hidden people groups and then recoil from the taxi-cab driver who takes them home, or ignore the 7-Eleven store merchant from whom they purchase gasoline, or a late night cup of coffee.

---

[2] Jerry L. Appleby, *Missions Have Come Home to America: The Church's Cross-Cultural Ministry To Ethnics* (Kansas City: Beacon Hill Press of Kansas City, 1986), 27.

[3] Charles Chaney, *Church Planting at the End of the Twentieth Century,* (Wheaton: Tyndale House Publisher, 1989), 19.

[4] Scott Nyborg, "Christ for the City - Miami: A Global Outreach", *Urban Mission,* Vol. 12. No. 3. Mar., 1995.

[5] David Hesselgrave, *Today's Choices for Tomorrow's Mission: An Evangelical Perspective on Trends and Issues in Today's Missions,* (Grand Rapids: Zondervan, 1988), 188.

[6] The 10/40 window refers to people who live between 10 degrees north of the equator and 40 degrees north of the equator from Spain to Japan.

Where's The Church?

Evangelical churches in America are predominantly English speaking, are middle class and have middle-class aspirations.[7] This is true whether the church is Native American, Asian American, Latino, Caucasian or African American. These congregations can win, and incorporate into their fellowships, some of the unreached millions of urban poor. But most effective evangelism among the unchurched occurs when the Good News is proclaimed by peers and is celebrated in comfortable cultural forms.

Two developments in the inner city during the past quarter century have increased the number of those unreached by the gospel, the urban unchurched.

1. Few Ethnic Churches Reach Cross-Culturally

With the passage of the 1965 Civil Rights Act, which struck down housing discrimination, over three and one half million middle-class African Americans moved out of the inner city,[8] including many church members and their pastors. The inner city thus lost a crucial anchor.[9] This second migration (see page 57) started the geographical and social separation of a strong middle class from the poor, who were left in the inner city.[10]

Today, many ethnic churches continue to meet in the inner city, but minister primarily to middle-class parishioners who have relocated out of the city. "Since the 1960's, 48% of the Black population of Atlanta has moved out of the central city into surrounding counties. The gradual emergence of two fairly

---

[7]   Harvie Conn, "Urban Mission," *Toward the 21st Century in Christian Mission,* (Grand Rapids: Eerdmans, 1993), 145.

[8]   Andrew Wiese, "Places of Our Own: Suburban Black Towns Before 1960," *Journal of Urban History* 19, no. 3 (May, 1993): 30.

[9]   William Julius Wilson, *The Truly Disadvantaged; The Inner City, The Underclass and Public Policy,* (Chicago: University of Chicago Press, 1987).

[10] Between 1970 and 1990 the percentage of Black families earning more than $50,000 increased 46%; the percentage of African Americans with college degrees doubled, as did the percentage of Black men holding white-collar jobs. Vanesa Williams, "Blacks, Too, Are Becoming Two Societies," *Philadelphia Inquirer,* 4 Apr. 1993, C1, C3.

distinct Black Americas along class lines—of two nations within a nation—has raised a serious challenge to the Black Church."[11] "The membership of the seven historic Black denominations is composed largely of middle-class members, with a scattering of support from poorer southern rural members. But Black pastors and churches have had a difficult time reaching the hard-core urban poor, the Black underclass, which is continuing to grow."[12]

Other minority churches also find it extremely difficult to cross cultural or economic lines in order to evangelize or minister to the poor who live around their sanctuaries. This leaves a large segment of the population unchurched, despite the physical presence of church buildings in urban neighborhoods.

2. The Flight Of The White Evangelical Church To The Suburbs

As cities became more populous and culturally complex, White evangelical churches followed their members who had relocated outside the city. Between 1970 and 1980, Chicago lost one third of its White citizens; St. Louis lost 27%; Los Angeles lost 16%.[13] Over one half of all urban churches are in transitional communities. Each year, 2000 urban churches disband or merge.[14] In the inner city, few White evangelical churches exist that can reach cross-culturally.

A Divided Church

Even if the Church had been near the urban poor, some question whether it could have ministered to people from different cultures, races, languages and classes because of the ongoing legacy of segregation and exclusion in the Church,

---

[11] One third of Black families live in poverty. Harvie M. Conn, *The American City and The Evangelical Church: A Historical Overview,* (Grand Rapids: Baker, 1994), 125.

[12] C. Eric Lincoln and Lawrence H. Mamiya, *The Black Church in the African American Experience,* (Durham: Duke University Press, 1990), 384.

[13] Charles Gloab and Theodore Brown, *A History of Urban America,* 3d. ed. (New York: Macmillan, 1983), 351.

[14] Earl Parvin, *Missions USA,* (Chicago: Moody Press, 1985).

which continues today.[15]

For example, one week after the Rodney King tapes aired, I preached in a predominantly White suburban church. Most worshipers there believed that if they knew all of the facts—if they had seen everything that occurred without the press editing and interpreting the tapes—there would have likely been a reasonable explanation of why the officers so violently subdued Rodney King. The police might have over-reacted, but Rodney King had broken the law. He probably deserved what he got.

The opposite assumption was made the following Sunday when I spoke at an historic Black church in Central Los Angeles. Worshipers there knew that this was not an isolated incident, but an all-too-normal response of excessive force in the minority community by the authorities.

If the perspective of the urban Christians had been heard by the suburban congregation, they might have suspected that the inner-city church was biased and liberal. But if the urban Christians had heard about the suburban believers' predisposition to trust the police, the urban Christians would have likely characterized their suburban brothers as ignorant (of the untrustworthiness of police among the poor), prejudiced and uncaring.

While both churches love Jesus, there is little communication between the two. Neither pastor and few of their members would recognize people from the other congregation if they passed each other at a UCLA basketball game.

The churches' responses to the King beating were more than two different opinions about the same incident. They revealed a deeper, far more serious gulf—two divergent world views, two contrasting sets of experiences and assumptions that influence how these congregations see life in America.

---

[15] The sin of segregation and exclusion did not begin in the American Church. Acts 10 and 11 reveal deep-seated racial prejudice as Peter, and the other leaders of the early Church, refused to associate with Gentiles, let alone believe that God could redeem them. God had to miraculously intervene through the baptism of the Holy Spirit before the pillars of the Church admitted, "So then, God has granted *even the Gentiles* repentance unto life."

Sunday Morning White[16]

Racial and cultural isolation, rooted in an absence of relationships, leads to division and suspicion. Prejudice is a function of ignorance fueled by a lack of communication. It leads to avoidance ("I don't want to be around them") and stereotyping ("They *always* act this way or do that"). Prejudice is sad in society, but tragic when it occurs within the body of Christ.

Racism has been part of the American Church for centuries. Beginning in 1619, most of the White Church exchanged its prophetic voice of justice and righteousness for an apologetic reflection of what the dominant culture wanted to hear, in spite of the ungodliness of the more popular message.

Ministers theologically justified the existence of Black slavery, dividing the "oneness of man" doctrine into the present and the hereafter, explaining that in the present Blacks were inferior. Faithful, obedient slaves would find equality with Whites in the next world.[17]

The Church misused Jesus and the gospel to justify discrimination, segregation, apartheid and extermination (genocide) in America. A Christian minister led an Indian massacre. Pre-Revolutionary War Quakers had segregated burial grounds. Puritan ministers owned slaves in Connecticut. And George Whitfield, the revivalist, fought to bring slavery to Virginia.[18]

Even after slavery was abolished, racism continued in the Church. The powerful Pentecostal movement, birthed through a Black man at Azusa Street in Los Angeles, eventually splintered into Black and White denominations. Whites presumably had a difficult time submitting to Black leadership.[19]

---

16 If I were an African American, the title of this section would be, "Sunday Morning Black."

17 Claud Anderson, *Black Labor White Wealth* (Edgewood, Md.: Duncan & Duncan, 1994), 73, 74.

18 UCLA Lecture Notes, The American Negro (History 176A, B) Dr. R. Takaki, 1966.

19 This division was not unique to Pentecostals. The African Methodist Episcopal Church split off from the Methodist Episcopal Church (now United Methodists) and the National Black Baptist Convention divided from the Baptists. Frank S. Mead, Revised by Samuel S. Hill, *Handbook of Denominations in the United States* (Nashville: Abingdon Press, 1990), 195.

Blacks were often denied due respect because they were perceived to lack a history, or to have failed to make a contribution to society. Legally, slaves had no past or future, so they were denied their place in history. Owners changed their slaves' names and refused to acknowledge their culture or history, leading to "historicide"—suppressing the slaves' memories of their past.[20] But the owners could not destroy the past.

I say *perceived* to have no history, because Africans were intimately involved in salvation history (Moses' wife, Zipporah; Jethro; and others) and were a powerful force in the early Church (Niger, Simon, Anasthasius, the Ethiopian eunuch, early Bible scholars from Carthage and Alexandria).[21]

African Americans have also contributed significantly to American society. Among other accomplishments too numerous to mention, they built the first clock in America, patented a sugar-refining process, developed 300 products created from the peanut, performed the first open-heart surgery and discovered how to make electricity from gas.[22]

Secular society attempted to legislate racial reconciliation (or inclusiveness) through mandatory integration in the workplace and in government. But ironically, the most natural place for racial reconciliation (inclusiveness) to happen, the Church, remained one of the last bastions of institutional segregation in America.

Rooted in a past when Whites refused to sit with Blacks (or other minorities) in God's house,[23] many congregations con-

---

[20] Orlando Patterson, *Slavery and Social Death: A Comparative Study*, (Boston: Harvard University Press, 1982).

[21] Lecture by Dr. Allan Callahan, Professor of New Testament at Harvard Divinity School at Westside Christian Fellowship, Santa Monica, California, 1996.

[22] Melvin Banks, *World Vision*, (Feb. - Mar., 1996), 14.

[23] In the 1780's in Philadelphia, the White Methodists permitted Negroes to worship with them provided the Negroes sat in a designated place in the balcony. On one occasion, when Negro worshipers occupied the front rows of the balcony, from which they had been excluded, the officials pulled them from their knees during prayer and evicted them from the church. The White Methodists from New York had a similar attitude. Soon separate Negro churches were formed.

In 1809, 13 Negro members of a White Baptist church in Philadelphia were dismissed and formed their own church. The earliest Negro religious institutions

tinue that sinful division today. The traditional White church may have less than 5% ethnic parishioners. Black, Brown and Asian members of these predominantly White congregations usually share the dominant culture of that church.

Few Black churches have more than one or two percent non-African-American worshipers. In Asian churches, few individuals attend who are not of that ethnicity.

Los Angeles reflects a meeting of the United Nations, yet for many churches, Sunday morning still remains the most segregated hour in the United States. When people of several races live on the same block, go to the same school, work and shop together and watch their children play in the same Little League, but worship separately according to their race, how can the Church claim that we are all *one* in Christ?[24]

Racism Slanders God

Believing that one race is inherently superior to others is idolatry, honoring the created above the Creator. A Christian racist is a polytheist, i.e., he worships Christ and his race.[25] Racism pejoratively judges God's creative action by saying some segments of humanity are defective, that God made a creative error. It then adds to the Bible, inferring that some races are victims of a double fall.[26]

---

emerged as a result of the rejection by White worshipers. Negro churches of virtually every denomination were the answer for a people who had accepted the White man's religion, even as the White man rejected his converts. *The Negro American* (Boston: Houghton, Mifflin & Company, 1966), 49.

[24] There are several notable exceptions where churches reflect their multi-racial community, but most congregations are still racially segregated. When confronted with this apparent contradiction most predominantly single-race churches explain that people from every race are welcome, they just do not come. Perhaps the Church is segregated because it has always been so. . .that is just the way it is. Perhaps it erected barriers of which it is unaware. One wonders if these explanations please God. Maybe we need to strategize how to disassemble those barriers and to purposefully blend our homogenous congregations racially—in obedience to Christ and as a witness to our neighbors.

[25] George B. Kelsey, *Racism and the Christian Understanding of Man*, (New York: Charles Scribner's Sons, 1965).

[26] The first fall is Adam's fall from grace. The second fall would be certain races dropping below others.

Racism denies our common humanity in creation and our belief that all people are made in the image of God. God's gift of image is an act of pure grace, a dignity God confers on all people equally. Racism denies the effectiveness of Jesus' reconciling work, through whose love all human diversities lose their divisive significance.[27] It falsely asserts that we find our importance in racial identity, rather than in Jesus.

Racism is sin. Tony Evans declared, "Unrepentant racists in churches—whether Black or White—need to be disciplined just like any other unrepentant sinners."[28] The racist must be confronted with a Christ who is love. A Christian loves because he has been, and is, loved. When a racist yields to Christ, his pride of racism is overcome "by faith in the Son of God, who loved (him) and gave Himself for (him)" (Galatians 2:20). Christ becomes "the way, the truth and the life" (John 14:6).

The Christian Church should not be divided by race or ethnicity. It should not be the big toe dragging behind the body politic. It troubles me to see White or Black denominations, or Associations of Christians with a racial adjective before their name, e.g. African, Mexican, Chinese or German Association of...[29] Emphasizing our differences, rather than celebrating our uniqueness together, leads to isolation, poor communication and misunderstanding, which bolsters continued suspicion and racial distrust.

Because the Church does not demonstrate the reconciling power of the gospel it declares, its message is losing credibility with our young people. Minority youth are forced to choose between fighting for the principles of <u>Brown vs. the Board of Education</u> (Supreme Court case mandating school integration), or reverting to Louis Farakhan's prejudicial demand of separate, but equal.

---

[27] Johannes Verkuyl, *Break Down the Walls* (Grand Raids, MI: Wm. Eerdmans Publishing Co., 1973).

[28] Promise Keepers Pastors' Conference in Atlanta, 1996.

[29] Minorities need to draw strength from one another in order to relate to different groups as peers. But the fact that "drawing strength" is still needed in the Church troubles me.

Even though Farrakhan is a racist who panders to despotic North African and Middle Eastern dictators and Islamic extremists, he is widely admired by Black youth in America. People forget his hate language and anti-Semitism because of his emphasis on self-reliance, Black pride, morality and a strong family. One Christian brother told me that Farrakhan *does* everything Christians *preach*.

The Church should offer an alternative of unity amid diversity for our youth. Before the Church can bring reconciliation to the alienated urban poor, it must heed the parable, "Physician, heal yourself" (Luke 4:34).

The Church must repent of its racism and intentionally promote racial, cultural and class reconciliation among its members. Then it can become a refuge for the needy, not derelict in its duty.

When the Church should have experienced its brightest hour (during the division following the King verdict) it was out of touch with the poor and alienated, and had not reconciled with itself.

Summary

The 1992 riots were caused by people's hopelessness stemming from:

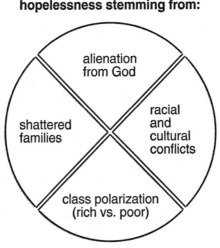

alienation from God

racial and cultural conflicts

shattered families

class polarization (rich vs. poor)

SECTION III
BEAUTY IN
THE MAKING:
A CHRISTIAN RESPONSE

The alienation that caused the 1992 riots, and continues today, seems unsolvable. A sinister demon could hardly have designed a more defeating scenario: the urban poor trapped in racial and cultural strife, watching their families dissolve, alienated from the middle and upper classes and yet yearning for that "Fresh Prince of Bel Air" lifestyle, and wondering if God or His Church even care.

I felt the same hopelessness in 1992 that I experienced in 1965 when Watts, a predominantly African-American community in Los Angeles, rioted. The despair of 1965 compelled me to do something. The explosion of 1992 motivated World Impact to refine our strategy and enlarge the scope of our vision.

The following testimonies of people touched by World Impact reveal how God uses ordinary Christians to bring healing to people and hope to whole communities.

Chapter VIII

The Birth of World Impact

When I first came to Watts, I knocked on the door of a federal housing project apartment. A 12-year-old boy peered out through a hole in the door.[1] He asked me what I wanted. I told him I wanted to tell him about Jesus. (I was using the direct approach to evangelism at the time.)

He said, "Wait a second. Let me ask my mom if I can come." Returning in a few moments with his 13-year-old brother, he said, "I can come, if he can come, too."

"That would be great," I responded. So the three of us set out together and picked up four more friends en route. At that first Bible club, those six boys and I made a deal. I promised to tell them about Jesus if they would tell me about life in the city. Although what I taught was new to them, there was no doubt that I learned more than they did that day.

After Bible club I started to walk toward my car. The six boys accompanied me, and asked me two questions that changed my life, "Mr. Keith, will you come back next week? And, if you do, would it be okay if we brought friends?"

I answered in the affirmative to both of those questions, got into my car and drove out of Watts, but my heart never left the inner cities of America.

---

[1] My early Watts experiences are chronicled in *They Dare To Love The Ghetto*.

The following Thursday afternoon, I drove down 103rd Street toward the housing projects, not sure how many boys would remember to show up for our newly-inaugurated Bible club. To my surprise, instead of finding six boys, there were 25. I heard one of them say, "See, I told you he'd come back." I guess they had debated whether or not I would brave it two weeks in a row.

The week after that there were 50 boys, then 70, and within six weeks, 100.

If you have ever taught at the junior-high age level, you understand why teaching 100 students by oneself in a Bible club was stretching the extremities of reason. So, I called a special meeting and said, "Listen, guys. No more brothers, nephews, uncles, friends or neighbors can join until someone drops out." And I started a waiting list.

I struggled as my waiting list rapidly increased. It broke my heart not to respond to every child who wanted to attend Bible club. Then the problem expanded. Parents started asking why I had not begun Bible clubs for the girls. And what about the older boys? And the younger children?

Every call bothered me. Still, there was nothing more I could do on my own. I had grown up in the First Baptist Church of Van Nuys, California. Even though thousands of people attended services every Sunday, on Monday we always went on visitation and invited more to come. How could any church, or ministry, be *full*? And then my quandary multiplied geometrically.

Watts occupies one square mile. Every corner of Watts has a federal housing project on it. Each person I knew seemed to have family in the other three housing projects. I began getting phone calls from relatives in these nearby projects asking me to start Bible clubs there: "Why don't you come here? We have children, nephews, nieces and cousins who need to learn about the Bible and want to have a Bible club, too." I did not know how to respond.

I talked to urban and suburban pastors asking, "How can you send scores of missionaries and thousands of dollars all around the world, and ignore the inner city of Los Angeles?" Most were supportive of my ministry, but none offered personnel. Finally, God gave me an idea.

Biola College was located a few miles down Imperial Highway from Watts. They had hundreds of students who needed Christian service assignments, and I had thousands of kids who needed to be served by Christians—what a fit!

But, since Watts had recently rioted, Biola had to weigh what the parents would say, how their trustees would respond and what their legal liability was, before they could make a commitment. After much prayer, I was invited to speak in Biola's chapel, share with their students what I had done and present an opportunity I had for them to minister.

Biola's chapel was held in a gymnasium. Students filled the bleachers on both sides and the folding chairs that covered the basketball court. I stood in front of my first college chapel and talked about the open door we had to reach children for Christ. I invited every student who was willing to help me teach Bible clubs weekly in an inner-city housing project to come to Marshburn Hall that evening.

That night 300 collegians filled Marshburn Hall! My heart beat with anticipation. I tried my best to train these volunteers how to teach Bible clubs in Watts. I stressed commitment. The college students had to come *every* week because their consistency would reflect the faithfulness of God. It did not matter if they had a late date, or had to study for an upcoming test. They needed to build strong relationships with their Bible-club children. These youngsters had to come first!

Unlike the Billy Graham or Luis Palau Crusades, we had no advance team to prepare for our initial thrust into Watts. However, it was hardly necessary to announce our coming. For in the late 1960s, Watts was primarily African American. Biola, on the other hand, was not.

So, when the big yellow buses loaded with Biola students rolled into the housing projects, no brass band was needed to signal our presence. Everyone knew we had arrived. Children ran to see these college students climbing out of the buses. That first week, 300 Biola volunteers came to Watts, and we had 3000 children in Bible clubs. If we would have had 500 college students, I am convinced that we could have had 5000 children in Bible clubs. (We limited Bible clubs to ten students for every teacher.) When the children sensed the collegians' love, care and attention, immediate friendships were formed.

The Biola students' exciting ministry taught me two important principles, which have stunning implications for the Church today:

1. Whoever spends even a *little* amount of time with inner-city children can have a great influence on them; and

2. Whoever spends the *most* time, wins. If every American Christian would build relationships regularly with two or three children from the city, the Church could have a massive influence on the next urban generation.

Chapter IX

The Early Years:
Evangelism

Watts is only one of many inner cities populated by the urban poor. But Watts was the community where God began to work in my life, and where His work led to establishing a ministry called World Impact. (See *Addendum A* for World Impact's purpose, and its biblical basis for ministry).

It was obvious that a segment of society torn apart by broken families, alcohol and drug abuse, violence, theft and fear needed spiritual revival. So I preached the Good News of Jesus, and recruited hundreds of others to join with me in sharing Christ's love with our inner-city neighbors.

Initially, we ministered primarily to children through Bible clubs. As the youngsters grew up, and their brothers, sisters and parents became interested in the gospel, our work expanded to entire families.

Had you observed our early ministry in Watts (and the start of every new ministry we have launched throughout Los Angeles and across the nation) you could have correctly summarized the beginnings of our outreach with one word: *"EVANGELISM."*

We define evangelism as "everything we say and do that reveals the love of God to our neighbors." This includes teaching the Bible to children, teenagers and adults; feeding a hungry youngster; walking an elderly, fearful woman to the store; relocating burned-out or evicted families; providing heat to freezing neighbors in winter; giving medicine to the sick; and just being there with a warm smile, a listening ear or a shoulder to cry on.

It did not take long to realize that three important ingredients enhanced the effectiveness of our evangelism: the live-in ministry, ministering to the whole person and ministering to the whole family.

The Live-In Ministry

Our missionaries, who minister in the city, live in the community where they serve. This is an extension of the Incarnation. When God had an important message to give to man, He became flesh and dwelt among us. Then we beheld His glory, that of the only begotten of the Father, full of grace and truth (John 1:14).

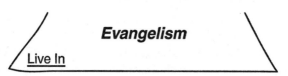

If I were called to be a missionary in Beirut, but intended to live in Jerusalem and commute, no doubt you would counsel, "If your ministry in Lebanon is going to be fruitful, you must live in Lebanon." To effectively minister in the inner city, one needs to live in the inner city. Living where we minister has three compelling benefits.

1. *Availability.* The inner city is a society in crisis. If you are only in the community from 8 a.m. to 5 p.m., Monday through Friday, you will miss much of the action and consequently, most of the teachable moments. Living in the community allows our missionaries to be available to their neighbors 24 hours a day.

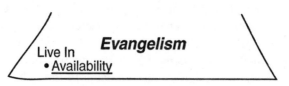

Virgil

Virgil Gray, a nine-year-old African-American boy, was one of the first people we met when we opened our Los Angeles women's home. When Virgil noticed our staff and volunteers renovating a house on his street, he decided to burglarize and ransack our garage "...primarily because they were White folks and I didn't want White folks living in my neighborhood."

A World Impact volunteer, Stan Gordon, caught Virgil. But, instead of turning him into the police, Stan turned Virgil into a higher authority, i.e., Stan invited Virgil to attend Bible club in the very house he had vandalized hoping he would meet the Lord there.

Virgil soon did accept Christ at Bible Club and became close friends with Gary Friesen, a 21-year-old World Impact staff member. Gary learned about life in the inner city through the eyes of Virgil while teaching Virgil to see life through the eyes of Jesus.

Gary heard about Virgil's abusive father, a heavy drinker who often beat Virgil's mother, Shirley. Virgil recalls waking up early in the mornings "...hearing my mother screaming. Somebody had thrown her up against the wall. My father would order me to go back to bed, but I wouldn't go. I used to cling to my mother. I remember the violence.

"My father said that I would never amount to anything, that I would be in jail before I was in high school. He said women were no good. Their only value was in having babies and making you money."

Shirley tried desperately to keep her family together against insurmountable odds. When Virgil was 12, she made the difficult decision to separate from her husband. This meant dividing the children among various relatives for a time.

Since Shirley had left Virgil's father against his will, he threatened to kill Shirley and the children. Virgil was terrified whenever he saw a car like his father's, fearing he would make good on his promise.

Gary comforted and helped Virgil when his family went without electricity for six months.[1] Virgil would stop by Gary's house after school full of questions about what the Bible had to say concerning his fears and struggles.

Virgil was eager to share his problems and pray about them. Gary's constant availability helped Virgil maintain his Christian commitment during his teen years, despite peer pressures and family struggles. Virgil eventually became a World Impact missionary.

Virgil's older brother Wendell, who did not attend Bible club, was not so fortunate. His father's threats and abuse drove Wendell to drugs and drinking, and then to sniffing paint and glue, which ruined his mind.

Virgil sadly recalls, "Years later, after I had become a missionary, *my* Bible-club students would sometimes make fun of homeless people. One day they saw Wendell and started joking about him. I told my guys that he *is* somebody's family, and I went over and hugged Wendell. He now lives in a mental hospital."

Robin

Robin was another person to whom we were *available*. One Christmas Eve, I received a phone call indicating that 17-year-old Robin, and her younger brother and sister, had been put out on the street with no place to live.

I learned that Robin's mother and father got married a month after Robin was born. The marriage did not last because Robin's father spent so much time in jail; he stole to support his heroin addiction. Robin has no memory of her father living with her. She does recall riding in a car while he participated in a burglary. Having children ride with him helped him avoid being stopped by the police.

---

[1] Virgil's family almost burned their house down with candles. We paid to get the electricity turned back on.

Through the witness and change of lifestyle in Robin's two sisters, Robin decided to begin attending Bible study at our single women's home. Six months later, while at a retreat with her Bible teacher, Ann Becker (now Dokken), 15-year-old Robin asked Jesus to come into her life and be her Savior. Her brother also started coming to Bible Study soon after that.

Robin spent a lot of time with our missionaries. She went to church with them, helped teach children's Bible clubs, spent the night in their homes and vacationed with them.

After Robin's family was cut off of welfare, they sometimes went without food, electricity and even water. When they were evicted, Robin's mother announced that she could no longer provide for her children. She could not locate their father. She called foster homes, but the children were too old for foster care.

Mary Thiessen, our women's director, suggested that Robin could live with her, and that Robin's brother could live with the single men on our staff. Robin lived with our single staff women for three-and-a-half years. During this time Robin finished high school, attended college and became a part of our staff family.

Robin's older sister joined the military. Her younger sister stayed with an uncle, and later lived with her mother in a storage shed until she entered our Women's Training Program in Portland, Oregon.

Had World Impact missionaries not *lived in the community*, they might have conducted excellent programs, but they would not have been on hand to demonstrate God's forgiveness to Virgil, God's provision to Shirley or God's mercy to Robin.[2]

2. *Modeling* is a second benefit of our live-in ministry. People understand the message of the gospel most clearly when they see it lived rather than just hear it spoken. We learn best by observing others.

---

[2] "We shared about our lives in this book to testify to the power, grace and glory of God. While our pasts are painful, our futures are bright because of Jesus. We pray our testimonies will encourage others trapped in poverty and raised in broken homes to believe in miracles. We also pray our stories will encourage members of the Church—Black, White, Asian and Hispanic—rich and poor—to actively be involved with people in our forgotten cities." --Virgil and Robin Gray.

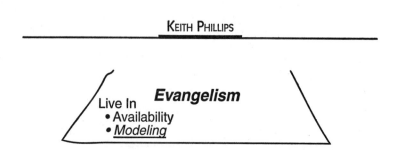

Many children and teenagers we teach have never lived with two godly parents who instruct and guide them. Boys who have no father to imitate have a poor conception of the Christian husband and father that God wants them to become. Girls with no father struggle to understand what a godly marriage should look like. Living a Christian lifestyle, whether married or single, is a crucial aspect of modeling for our missionaries.

In 1988, Virgil and Robin were married. Virgil confesses, "I feared that I would become like my father and devastate my wife and my son. Watching Gary Friesen and the other staff men take their sons to ball games and do homework with them helped me see that I could become a godly father and make my family my priority. I learned...

• that I could be committed to one woman for the rest of my life. This was the most important thing I discovered.

• the priority of my family. The concept of parents spending time with their children was totally foreign to me. Actually, at first I resented how much time a fellow missionary, Kim Seebach, spent with his wife, and how important his family was to him. I was jealous since it had not been like that in my family. For Kim, God was first; family second; ministry third. Now when Robin and I sit at the dinner table with our children, we turn away other youngsters from our door who want to come in, so we can have our family time.

• the value of a woman, to hold Robin in high esteem. My past dictated that if I had a wife, I would be under a lock and chain. World Impact's staff men changed that perception. Having a Christian wife has enhanced my life and ministry. My family is a miracle of God and a witness to His love.

"I remember neighborhood kids saying to Robin, 'What are you going to do when Virgil finds a better-looking woman?' They expected me to be unfaithful.

"One little girl in Watts saw me change a diaper and do dishes. She asked, 'Why are you doing woman's work? A man's supposed to lift weights, watch sports and drink beer. Men don't look after kids like you do!' God taught me a lot through watching Christian men."

3. *Identification.* In addition to being available and modeling the Christian life, living where we minister helps us identify with our neighbors. When World Impact missionaries move into a community, the distinction between "you" and "me" blurs into an "us." Reservations about our motives dissipate, and paternalism fades as we address "our" problems and needs.

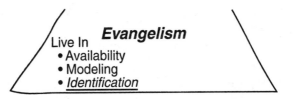

When Robin became engaged to Virgil, she began ministering with him in Watts. Virgil remembers, "I had no desire to go to Watts. It was scary, known as the poorest place in Los Angeles. The needs and burdens were overwhelming. When I was young, I called Watts the 'armpit' of Los Angeles."

Living in Watts during the gang war of 1993 fostered an identification that otherwise could never have been achieved. No one walked outside at night: the street lights had been shot out. Virgil never let his children sleep in the front bedroom—the holes in the wall testified that too many bullets had lodged there.

Virgil recalls, "One evening, when I drove my students home from Bible club, guys with walkie-talkies were on every corner in black camouflage, waiting to ambush a rival gang if they came. A man pointed a shotgun right at our van. One child opened the van door and said, 'Don't shoot, it's me.' The guy ordered him to get into his house quickly." That evening Virgil told me at staff fellowship, "You almost lost me today," explaining that his life had been in the sights of a gun.

Later that night as Virgil lay in bed, he heard gunshots in front of his house. His neighbor, Rodney, who was getting in his car to go to work, was shot twice in the arm and several times in the legs. He was gasping for air. Virgil got his clothes on and rushed outside to help. He talked to Rodney and tried to keep him awake until the ambulance came. Later, Rodney's legs had to be amputated.

A week earlier, someone had run through Virgil's yard and shot and killed their dog. Virgil had to drag her out of the yard. Once Virgil was playing with Bible-club children when a car drove by and started shooting. They lay on the ground until he drove off. Another time, some children told Virgil that a man was lying in the parking lot, dead. That was the first time Virgil had seen a dead man. Later, a policeman was shot in the leg near Virgil's home.

Living where they ministered allowed Virgil and Robin to identify with the fears, stress and unpredictability of the city. They spoke with authority when they taught their neighbors that God could bring peace, joy and healing to Watts. Jesus said, "You are the salt of the earth. You are the light of the world. Let your light shine before men, that they may see your good deeds and praise your Father in heaven" (Matthew 5).

Ministry To The Whole Person

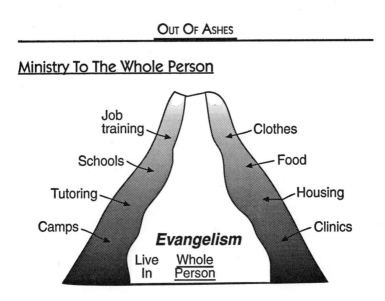

As we declared the gospel, we naturally began to demonstrate its implications.

If Virgil's hard-working mother, Shirley, needed assistance, she felt free to call World Impact missionaries. When Shirley's toilet clogged up, flooding her basement with sewage, our Los Angeles Director, Fred Stoesz, led a group of staff in wading through the waste to repair the clogged pipes and restore normal plumbing. When Shirley's car broke down, Kim Szalay, one of our missionaries, fixed it. When Shirley's roof leaked, the staff repaired it. When Shirley could not afford a bus pass to get to work, we purchased one for her. When Shirley did not have enough food for her eight children, we provided it.

As a result of seeing the gospel lived out, Shirley accepted Christ and began attending a weekly Bible study conducted by our staff women. She matured in her faith and soon started to reach her neighbors for Christ. Virgil's older brother, Ron, also accepted Christ and began growing in his faith.

As our staff grew, and the number of people we ministered to increased, our organization committed to further demonstrate the gospel that we declared.[3] Our holistic ministry includes Christian schools, job training and camps. (See *Addendum B*).

---

[3]   Our self-help compassion ministries are described in my book, *No Quick Fix*.

Ministry To Whole Families

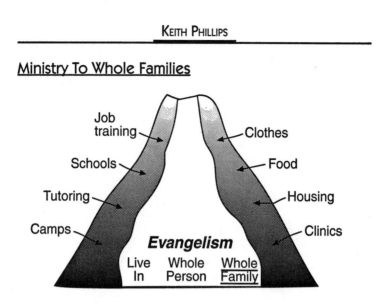

For practical, missiologically sound and biblical reasons, we started our urban ministry by focusing on children.

1. Children are receptive to new people and to the gospel. We could gather at least 100 youngsters for Bible club in most housing projects in America. As we love and care for the children, when they discover we love Jesus, so will they.

2. Children are an effective and quick way to learn about a new culture. If you want to know what makes a people group tick, listen to their children. They are open, vulnerable and frank.

3. Ministering to children gives teenagers, parents and neighbors an opportunity to watch how we treat their youngsters, to observe our motives, and to learn our reason for being in the city.

4. In a society of broken families, ministering to children builds future leaders for the Church. While single mothers, whose children have different fathers, can make their personal peace with God, marital fidelity is essential for the long-term stability of the urban Church. Children who know and live out this standard will become God's leaders.

Children who learn to follow Jesus early in life will hopefully marry Christian spouses later and establish godly homes. It is crucial to reach children for Christ before they are 12 years old, when they can become pregnant or can get someone else pregnant.[4] Most Christians alive today accepted Christ by age 12.

Gary Friesen confirmed the importance of ministry to children after recently hosting Virgil and Robin, and their three delightful children, in his home: "I was struck by how God has made Virgil into a caring husband and father in spite of his past, without a loving father in his home. I was touched as I watched Virgil put his children to bed by telling them the Old Testament story of Joshua and Caleb, which I assumed was a request from Virgil's son, whose name is Kaleb.

"As I think back on how fearful Virgil was of his earthly father, I am thankful for the way that God has revealed Himself to Virgil as a perfect, loving, heavenly Father. Virgil has a strong love for God and a growing desire to serve and worship Him. I praise God for His work in Virgil's life and for the way He is using Virgil in his family, and in the lives of other young men from the city."

5. Children provide direct access to the home. If children want to pray, memorize scripture or go to church, many parents will follow. When adults realize that someone else loves their children, they appreciate and want to affirm that relationship.

Virgil accepted Christ in Bible club when he was nine. His witness led to the conversion of his mother and older brother. After two years of discipleship training at our Kansas Ranch, Virgil returned to Los Angeles and led worship in World Impact's Celebration Church. Then he married Robin. They served as missionaries in Watts, and now disciple young people from the inner city at our Southern California camp.

Virgil's older brother, Ron, pastors the Celebration Christian Church, a World Impact Church plant. Virgil's nieces, nephews and cousins are in Bible clubs, teen Bible studies and our Los Angeles Christian School. Some have begun ministering to others. From evangelizing a single child, an extended family has been impacted for Christ.[5]

---

[4]   Thousands of premarital pregnancies have been, and can be, prevented by pre-teen conversions and Christian discipleship.

[5]   The Grays are one of hundreds of families that God has transformed through World Impact's ministry.

After our initial focus on children, we expanded our outreach to entire families. We strengthen, teach and equip parents through Bible studies, English classes, fellowship, choirs, camping, parenting classes and planting churches.

Evangelism characterizes World Impact's beginning thrust into our inner cities. But once people accept Jesus, they then need Christian nurture.

Chapter X

The Middle Years:
Christian Nuture

When people accept Jesus as their Savior they need to learn how to feed themselves spiritually. We call this *"FOLLOW UP."*

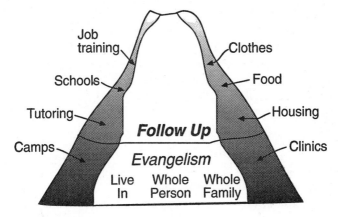

In 1975, my wife, Katie, became pregnant with our first child. I had promised Katie that I would not be off preaching in Chicago, Detroit, St. Louis, Wichita or some other exotic place and miss this blessed event. To back that up, I blocked off an entire month on my schedule before the due date, and a month after the due date, to be sure that I would be in Los Angeles.

On Sunday, July 13, 1976, I was preaching in a rural Mennonite church in Kansas. That afternoon, I flew to Newark. This was three days before "that blocked-off month" was to begin.

When I got to Newark, as was my custom, I phoned Katie to let her know where I was staying. She immediately suggested that I should take the first plane home. I pointed out to her that the previously-agreed-to month did not begin for another three days. She was *very* unimpressed, and after a brief conversation, I caught the next plane home.

When I arrived at the Los Angeles airport, I called home, but there was no answer. So I phoned my office. When I spoke to my secretary, I asked her if Katie had gone to the hospital and delivered.

My secretary said, "Yes, but are you sitting down?"

I said, "Are Katie and the baby healthy?"

My secretary responded, "Oh, yes. But are you sitting down?"

When I asked, "Did we have a boy or a girl?" she responded, "Two boys!" Then I sat down.

After the doctor had comforted me for about an hour, he explained that when you have one-month premature twins, they have to be fed every two hours, whether they are hungry or not.

I am convinced that from the very beginning, Joshua and Paul could communicate with each other. Joshua always wanted to be fed at midnight; Paul at 1:00 a.m.; Joshua at 2:00 a.m.; Paul at 3:00 a.m...

I soon discovered that right after we fed Paul, we had to go through a procedure that we affectionately called diapering. Then we could rock him back to sleep again. And just about the time Paul was asleep, it was Joshua's turn!

It does not take a wild imagination to understand that after going through this procedure 24 times every day for six weeks, Katie and I were a bit tired.

So, let's pretend that six weeks into the new lives of Joshua and Paul, I propped these splendid young men up against the couch and looked at them with all the seriousness that I could muster and said, "I know you are intelligent. I have been watching you, and you have been staring intently at every step of this procedure. You probably know it better than I do. Meanwhile, your mother and I are fatigued, and need to get away for the weekend...*alone.*

"But don't worry, because I have written out explicit instructions: how to feed yourself, how to make your formula, how to change your diapers, what symptoms to look out for...and I have left the phone number of our motel at the bottom of the page. So, if you have any questions, you can call.

"What do you say?" Since they were both nodding their heads up and down and grinning, I took that to be a response in the affirmative.

Now, let's suppose that Katie and I actually left Joshua and Paul, six weeks old, all by themselves for a weekend. What would have happened? I am not sure about your city, but in Los Angeles, they throw you in jail for that kind of thing. It is called "child abandonment."

Yet all too often, when the Church of Jesus Christ looks at the inner city, it is content to do just what I have described. We have a one-week evangelistic blitz, and then we leave.

Or, if we are terribly convicted, we take an offering and send 100 children from the housing projects to camp for the summer, stuff them full of the gospel, meticulously record their decisions, report to our church about the miraculous revival that took place and toss the youngsters back into the projects and yell, "God bless you! Hope everything works out okay. Here is a great six-week follow-up course. If you have any questions, be sure and phone." Then we wonder why on earth, next year, when we go back, there is no lasting fruit.

God began to convict us that with the privilege of being part of the birthing process comes the implied responsibility to stick around for the nurturing.

At the point of Joshua and Paul's conception, I had no idea what was involved in raising twin boys. But that did not take me off the hook. Today, 20 years later, Joshua and Paul weigh over 200 pounds and stand more than six feet tall. They have been trained how to feed themselves physically and spiritually.

In the same sense, when we lead people to the Lord, God expects us to nurture these young believers, even if we are at first afraid and do not know how. It is not enough to send them a weekly correspondence course, or to give them our phone number in case they have questions. Our physical presence—our availability, modeling and identification—are essential so that new converts can learn how to pray; how to study, memorize and meditate on God's Word; and how to worship the Lord. (See *Addendum A*).

This is not a six- or ten-week course. It may take years. But if God uses us to lead people to Christ, we are responsible to equip these new Christians to feed themselves spiritually.

DISCIPLESHIP

Once believers have been equipped to feed themselves spiritually and are living the Christian life, they need to teach others what they have learned (II Timothy 2:2).

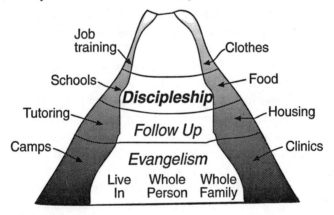

Provides Hope

This teaching of others, discipleship, gives us hope for reaching our inner cities for Christ; the kind of practical help without which focusing on the millions of lost could cause discouragement. Allow me to explain. Let's say God used me to lead one person to Christ this year. If I met with this new convert weekly to pray, memorize scripture and study God's Word, if we held each other accountable and came to church together, something extraordinary could happen.

Next year, the new convert and I could both lead one additional person to Christ, and invest in them. If we each continued to lead one new person to the Lord every year, and trained those individuals to join with us in teaching others to teach others, in 33 years I would have directly invested in 33 people (a reasonable task for any Christian). And, together with those I discipled, I would have reached the entire population of the world for Christ.[1]

Christ's message came wrapped in His method; multiplication is much quicker than addition. Discipleship is God's chosen method for passing the baton from one generation to the next.

Without Christ's method of making disciples (investing in the few, and teaching them to teach others, which leads to massive multiplication) we get discouraged, bitter, angry, and maybe even quit. But Christ's method sustains hope. And mathematically, Christians in the inner cities are several generations into this strategy of making urban disciples!

Assures Quality

Throughout salvation history, mentors have trained their students so well that their pupils have donned the cloak of leadership. For example, Moses trained Joshua, Elijah trained Elisha, and Christ adopted discipleship as His method for training His future apostles. Later, Barnabas trained Paul, and Paul trained Timothy and the others who joined with him in spreading the gospel. Like our predecessors in the faith, our focus is on discipling servant leaders.

Discipleship develops indigenous Christian leaders. New believers gain practical experience through observing and working alongside mature Christians, while receiving theological education, spiritual guidance, instruction and training within the local body. Disciples progress from being understudies, to co-laboring as leaders, to teaching new believers.

---

[1] See the Chart on page 23 of my book, *The Making of a Disciple*.

CHURCH PLANTING[2]

At World Impact, evangelism, follow up and discipleship eventually led to planting churches where new believers can grow in Christ.

After 25 years in the inner city, many of us asked, "Has the energy, efforts and focus of our lives in urban American been worthwhile? Have we been successful?" Those questions forced us to define success, which was a difficult exercise.

We remembered that our purpose in coming to the inner city was not just to help the less fortunate, but to *set people free!* Beginning community-owned and-operated businesses was

---

[2] The *volcano* you have been watching form (above) describes how World Impact's dynamic inner-city ministries of evangelism, follow up, discipleship and church planting are supported by schools, job training, camping and other ministries of compassion. A volcano has two separate, but complementary, parts–the hot inner core and the structured outer cone. If a volcano loses its hot inner core it becomes extinct. Without a strong outer cone, it splatters aimlessly, or blows itself to bits (see *Addendum C*).

good, but was not enough. Building houses for the homeless was admirable, but did not necessarily liberate people. Medical clinics and shelter ministries demonstrated God's compassion and mercy, but in and of themselves did not empower the poor to realize lasting change in their communities.

We had taught thousands of children, teenagers and adults in weekly Bible clubs and adult Bible studies. We had operated Christian schools, job-training programs, a medical/dental clinic and Christian camps. We had fed the hungry, clothed the needy and cared for the lonely.

While the impact of these ministries was great (lives were changed; families were healed; neighborhoods were improved), none of them catapulted us toward realizing our vision of taking our cities for Christ. The cities were still teeming with sin, enslaved by Satan and spinning farther and farther away from God.

After much prayer, study, discussion and contemplation, we concluded that the best way to make God known in the inner cities was to **"evangelize and equip the urban poor to minister to the urban poor."** That defined success for World Impact.

The fastest and most effective way to accomplish that objective is to plant culturally-conducive evangelical churches, which also thirst to fulfill the Great Commission (Matthew 28:18-20). Congregational discipleship, where each new church feels responsible to plant other churches, which will in turn birth additional church bodies, is the key to empowering the urban poor, and taking our cities for God.

If God could use us to plant 1000 healthy bodies of believers among the urban poor in South-Central Los Angeles (and in many other urban areas), the impact in a decade would be phenomenal! Why? Because this is the only solution that will heal the wounds of the Los Angeles riots and prevent future eruptions.

No government policy, no political white paper, no newspaper editorial nor television commentary practically explains how people from different races, cultures and classes can be reconciled with their neighbors. But God's Word does! **As men and**

women from different racial, ethnic and cultural groups are reconciled to God (Romans 5:1), they can then be reconciled with each other (as Jews and Gentiles did in the early Church). Koreans will embrace African Americans, Whites will honor Native Americans and Jesus will be preeminent!

The distinction of Christianity from all of the other great religions is not that it has:

- A rule book, or ethics manual, teaching you how to live. It does, but so do Buddhism and Hinduism.
- A global evangelical mission, with guidelines on how to minister. It does, but so does Islam.

The uniqueness of Christianity is the romance of God with His people. Before creation, God was planning to woo, or to call, a people from every ethnicity to be His Bride. God promised Abraham, that He would include all peoples (Genesis 12:1-3).

Amazingly, the Lord wants us to participate in preparing His Bride (expanding the Church). It *will* happen. The only question is whether or not we will be part of God's plan. And there is no better place to find the diversity God desires for His Bride than in our inner cities.

The Bible, after Genesis 12, records God's actions to fulfill His promise of bringing all nations into the Bride of Christ. The Old Testament law leads us to Christ and makes provision for the Gentiles. The Prophets foretell Christ's coming and ministry to non Jews (Isaiah 9:1,2). Christ's Incarnation, culminating at the Cross, provides for a universal multi-cultural Bride (Ephesians 2:11-22). The Great Commission commands us to teach all peoples because the end will not come until every ethnic group hears (Matthew 24:14). God's promise to Abraham will be fulfilled when "every nation, tribe, people and language" stand before Christ (Revelation 7:9)!

Chapter XI

Today:
Planting Urban Churches

Church planting is the most effective way to minister in our inner cities. *Becoming part of the Church—having a relationship with Jesus and with His followers—is the antidote to alienation.* God ordained the Church; it is the only institution that empowers the poor and sets them free! But coming to grips with the need for World Impact to plant churches required a journey of 25 years. Let me explain why it took us so long!

A Vision Develops

I grew up under the influence of Youth For Christ, where we channeled every new believer into an existing church. So when 16-year-old Jewel accepted Jesus in a Bible club on a vacant lot in Watts, we sent her to a local church, believing that she would be incorporated into that fellowship. But like so many other new Christians, Jewel said, "I do not fit in."

Initially, we did not understand. Jewel had a hard time explaining why, but we took her at her word.

Most churches would have gladly posted a sign over their door saying, "Whosoever will, may come." But usually, there was an additional, invisible sign that stated, "... as long as you are like us."

Few members were aware of the invisible sign, but visitors saw it immediately. They *knew* if they *fit*, if there was a cultural match. People who did not feel comfortable because of dress, class, language or ritual, seldom returned.

We knew that Jewel needed to attend church. That was never a question. But since she did not fit into a neighborhood church, we brought her, along with scores of other inner-city teens, to the churches where our staff felt comfortable—often in the suburbs.

In retrospect, most of these urban teenagers came to these middle-class churches because they wanted to please us and be with us. They doubtlessly felt culturally estranged by the worship style, and rarely, if ever, saw any hope of becoming an integral, contributing part of the church they attended. They were *going* to church (often out of their community) instead of *being* the Church.

In the meantime, World Impact was having Staff Fellowship meetings on Wednesday nights in missionary homes in South-Central Los Angeles. All of our staff, along with their spouses and children, ate, worshiped and praised God together, and prayed for each other and those in our ministry. The biblical teaching was a highlight for many of us.

Before long, people to whom we ministered asked if they could come to Fellowship. They, too, wanted to pray, worship God, have fellowship, study and eat together with us.

I understood the new Christians' desire to fellowship and worship with people in their community with whom they felt comfortable; yet our missionaries needed a time alone. So I said that Fellowship was for staff only; it was a *staff meeting*.

I was convinced that people we led to the Lord needed to join a church. However, I had not thought of our staff as a "church," and starting *new* churches was a foreign concept to me.

But the new believers persisted, so before long, we agreed to have a "celebration service" on Saturday evenings for our teens and neighbors. I made sure that everyone knew it was not "church" (after all, there seemed to be a plethora of inner-city churches). The last thing I thought we needed was more churches.

I had grown up Baptist, and there were Baptist churches all over. I could not understand why new believers would feel uncomfortable in a Baptist church. But my understanding was not the issue—they did not feel comfortable.

In spite of my reluctance, quasi-churches began springing up in our ministries from Watts to Newark. When new believers accepted Jesus, they desired to worship God with others in their neighborhood.

Before long, the worshipers asked, "Why can't we move our service to Sunday morning like everyone else?" My initial response was, "We are not a church." But after relentless questions, and much contemplation, I said, "We can meet on Sunday, but we will not call it 'church:' we will call it 'Celebration.'" So new believers from the city began worshiping together on Sunday morning...and later called it Celebration Church!

A Difference in Culture

I did not understand why new Christians seldom fit into local churches primarily because I was looking at the inner city in terms of color, ethnicity and race. East Los Angeles was mostly Mexican; Central and South-Central Los Angeles were predominantly African American. I mistakenly assumed that new Christians would be ministered to by *any* church composed predominantly of their race, but to my surprise, some people felt very out of place in certain churches even though they were the same race as the majority of the congregation.

It took me several years to realize that the issue was not "color" but "culture." The following diagram helped me understand the inner city in terms of culture.[1]

The dominant culture in the United States is Anglo-Saxon Protestant (ASP). This is no longer the majority culture, but it influences everyone who lives here. There are numerous subcultures, e.g., German American, Catholic American, Jewish American and Italian American to name a few.

---

[1] None of us like to be stereotyped. The purpose of the diagram is not to box in any person but to understand the cultural dynamics at work within and between racial groups; dynamics that have specific application for reaching the unchurched urban poor.

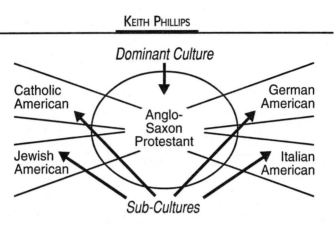

The urban culture has four major components: African American, Hispanic American, Anglo and Asian American. Each group is roughly divided into three subcultures noted as C_1, C_2 and C_3 (see the following diagram).

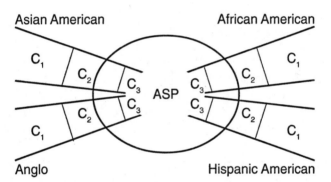

Let me use the African-American group as a cultural example. The C_3 African American *lives, works* and has been *educated* in the Anglo-Saxon Protestant (ASP) world (see diagram below). On the diagram, she is surrounded on three sides by the dominant culture.

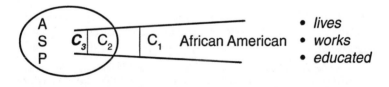

In Los Angeles, that could mean that she lives in Beverly Hills, works on Wilshire Boulevard and was educated at the University of Southern California. She has become part of the dominant culture. She could be an athlete, doctor, entertainer, engineer, attorney, politician or businessperson. She might be a proponent of Black power, but she wages her war for human rights from Beverly Hills.

The C_2 African American is bicultural.[2] His culture is dissected down the center (see below). Normally he lives in the inner city, but he works or is educated in the ASP world.

In Los Angeles, he might live in Watts but attend the University of Southern California. Or, he might live in South Central and work on Wilshire Boulevard. The C_2 African American is a talented individual who has learned to adapt to, and function effectively in, whichever culture he finds himself.

The C_2 person walks, speaks and dresses one way at work and another way at home. His actions, thinking, stature and the way he carries himself change as his environment changes.

The C_1 African American lives, works and is educated in the inner city (see below). His education may be formal or informal, obtained on the streets. However, his street education serves him well—he learns how to keep himself alive and how to provide for his immediate needs.

---

[2] The apostle Paul was bi-cultural. He was a Jew by family; a Greek by town. He spoke Greek as well as Hebrew. He was a circumcised Jew and a Roman citizen.

Let me illustrate. The first year I was in Watts, I was walking down 103rd Street with three friends. Suddenly, one teenager yelled, and another guy shoved me to the ground. A moment later a bullet whistled over my head. As I brushed myself off, I looked at these friends in amazement and asked how they knew that a gun was going to be fired. They laughed at me and said, "You mean you've got an education from UCLA and you can't even hear a gun cocking?" In certain environments, some kinds of education are more important than others.

Language: An Indicator Of Assimilation

For new immigrants (primarily Asian and Hispanic) language is a good indicator of their degree of assimilation into the dominant culture. For example, a C_3 Hispanic American speaks fluent English, but may speak little or no Spanish. He works, lives and is educated in the dominant culture. He has no intention of returning to his native land and has adopted the views and values of the dominant culture.

A C_2 Hispanic American is bi-cultural and bi-lingual (often speaking Spanish at home, but English at work or at school). She lives in East Los Angeles (the inner city) but works or receives her education in the dominant culture. Her roots may still be in her homeland (she occasionally has passing thoughts of returning home if all does not work out in the United States). If Mexican, she celebrates *Cinco de Mayo* with equal or more vigor than the Fourth of July. She likely thinks in Spanish, wants to read important legal documents in Spanish and worships God most comfortably in Spanish.

A C_1 Hispanic American lives, works and is educated in the barrio. He might speak broken English, but uses Spanish most of the time. He may be a migrant worker, adapting to the dominant culture enough to survive, e.g., he knows not to cross the street on a red light, understands the difference between the men's and women's restrooms and realizes that when a siren blares he should get his car out of the way.

In Which Culture Is The Church?

As you look at the culture diagram, in which culture do you think most inner-city churches fall? People usually agree that most churches fit squarely in the C_2 culture, and are often striving to move toward the C_3 culture. Even though many urban Anglos, African Americans, Asian Americans and Hispanic Americans are C_1, C_1 evangelical churches are few and far between, leaving millions of people unchurched.

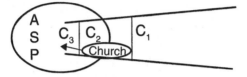

Looking back on my original experience with urban churches, the cultural differences made C_1 believers hesitant about joining C_2 congregations. The C_1 Christians felt out of place. They did not wear the appropriate clothing and did not know the rituals or enjoy the length of the service. C_1 believers found the cultural change so great that integrating was difficult.

It would be a great cultural leap for a Baptist, like me, to feel immediately comfortable in a liturgical service, like those enjoyed by the Lutherans or Episcopalians. Yet neither culture is better than the other. Both have great value.

Culturally-Comfortable Churches Needed

World Impact ministers to the urban poor, who are primarily in the C_1 culture. We were not initially successful in developing great numbers of indigenous leaders in the inner city because we made one of two mistakes:

1. If a C_1 accepted Christ, we encouraged her to go to a C_2 church (change cultures) in order to grow in her Christian faith.

$$C_1 \xrightarrow{change} C_2 = \text{Christian}$$

2. Or if a C_1 became a Christian and had great potential, we encouraged him to go to a school like Wheaton College or

Gordon Seminary to prepare himself to minister. However, few C_3 institutions equip their students to minister *in the inner city.*

$$C_1 \xrightarrow{\text{change}} C_3 = \text{Christian}$$

Although we did not specifically say it, we strongly implied that it was impossible to be a C_1 and a Christian. We left the C_1 believer with no option other than to change cultures if he were going to become a mature believer. We did not understand that we had fallen into the Apostle Peter's trap of forcing a believer to conform to a culture instead of conforming to Christ (Galatians 2:11-14).

This situation parallels what the New Testament Church faced when the Apostle Paul started to evangelize Gentiles. Initially, the Jerusalem Church assumed that a Gentile had to become a Jew (be circumcised and observe the Jewish dietary laws) in order to become a Christian.

$$\text{Gentile Believer} \xrightarrow{\text{change}} \text{Jew} = \text{Christian}$$

But the Holy Spirit must have caused uneasiness about this mandatory cultural change for church membership because the church leaders called the Council of Jerusalem to determine the propriety of forcing a Gentile to become a Jew in order to become a Christian (Acts 15).

At Jerusalem, the Holy Spirit revealed to these Christian leaders that it was unnecessary for a Gentile to change cultures in order to become a Christian: a Gentile did not have to become a Jew in order to be accepted into the Church. God meets people in the culture in which He finds them.

$$\text{Gentile Believer} \xcancel{\xrightarrow{\text{change}} \text{Jew}} = \text{Christian}$$

It *was* possible to be both a Gentile and a Christian.

$$\text{Gentile Believer} = \text{Christian}$$

The C_1 culture is neither more sinful nor more godly than the C_2 or C_3 cultures—God and His gospel are culturally neutral. While the gospel works in all cultures, the economic status of C_1 believers, and their acceptance by society in general, closely parallels the status, and society's reception, of early Christians.

This biblical principle of cultural neutrality, which encouraged indigenous leadership in every culture, allowed the gospel of Christ to become universally applicable. It set the stage for the Church's worldwide missionary efforts. Soon Philip and Paul began to evangelize and plant churches among non-Jewish peoples who had never heard of Christ.[3] Their example is relevant to our inner-city ministry today.

Just as it was wrong to force a Gentile (an African, Greek or Roman) to become a Jew in order to follow Jesus, it is equally wrong to force, either consciously or subconsciously, a C_1 African American, Hispanic American, Asian American or Anglo to change cultures—to become a C_2 or C_3—in order to become a believer.

$$C_1 \xrightarrow{\text{change}} C_2 \;\; C_3 = \text{Christian}$$

New Christians must have the option of remaining C_1 and being Christians.

$$C_1 = \text{Christian}$$

If all C_1 believers leave their culture, the C_1 culture will never be influenced for Christ. No Christians will be left there to reproduce themselves and teach others. For the Church to gain a stronghold among the urban poor, C_1 believers must stay and transform the neighborhoods where they were living when they met Jesus.

We encourage new believers to worship in evangelical C_1 churches if they exist in the community. Or, if C_1 converts choose to change cultures and become part of a biblically-sound C_2 or

---

[3] Paul (a C_2) was adept at crossing cultures and facilitating multiple cultures to become one in Christ. Romans 16:22, 24 say, "I, Tertius (a slave, whose name was 'Three' [Romans numbered their slaves]—a C_1, who physically wrote this letter), greet you in the Lord. (24)Erastus (C_3), who is the city's director of public works (City Treasurer of Corinth), and our brother Quartus (a slave whose name was 'Four') send you their greetings." Seasoned World Impact missionaries, and their children who grow up in the inner city, often find themselves becoming C_2's as well, for Christ's sake.

C_3 church, we support them, but they must not be forced to change cultures in order to become Christians.

However, in the absence of those options, World Impact disciples indigenous C_1 leaders and plants inner-city churches. This allows C_1 Christians to remain in their culture, live for Christ there, and reach many more C_1 city dwellers for our Lord.[4]

A Dream Becomes A Reality

Once we understood that we should plant culturally-comfortable churches for the urban poor, we committed to studying missiology and Church history in order to learn from others who had planted churches among the urban poor. We then began to pray that God would bless us to effectively plant thousands of churches in our inner cities.

Transitioning from whole-person discipleship to church planting was a bud maturing into a blossom for World Impact, the natural culmination of 25 years of service. Every ministry we have launched (Bible clubs, Bible studies, job training, clinics, housing, schools, camps, etc.) naturally leads to, and is enhanced by, the planting of healthy, indigenous bodies of Christ among the urban poor.

The Church, the Bride of Christ, is the only place where fruit from urban evangelism can be secured. Further, incorporating believers into Christ's body is the only way to *set people free*.

Church plants have begun in several of the cities where we minister. Victories have been won as people and neighborhoods have been changed. However, we are not satisfied. We are motivated to press forward from a few communities to entire cities. We expect to see an explosion of new churches guided by dynamic, urban leaders.

---

[4] God calls *some* C_1 Christians to become C_2's in order to equip them for missionary work. They are the exception, not the rule.

Summary: World Impact's strategy to make God known (Matthew 28:18-20).

1. Evangelism (Colossians 4:3-6; II Timothy 4:2).
2. Follow Up (I Timothy 4:12; II Timothy 2:2; Romans 1:11).
3. Discipleship (Matthew 28:18-29; John 8:31).
4. Church Planting (I Corinthians 3:10; Acts 13, 16).

Chapter XII

Preparing For The Future:
A Missions Organization

Kim was stunned when I told her, "God will forgive you. He loves you more than you love yourself." This 16-year old gangster had robbed, beaten and abused people for years. But now she was tired of lying, cheating and running. She wanted a way out. She needed a Savior.

Kim's eyes welled up with tears as she began to comprehend that what God had already done for her was something that she could not do for herself. He had paid the penalty for her sins.

Kim prayed with such sincerity—confessing and repenting of her sins, asking Jesus to be her Savior, thanking Him for His love and promising to love Him. She was so excited, wanting to tell the girls she ran with about Christ.

If there is a better job than being a missionary, I want to know about it. A missionary tells people who have never heard, the best news they will ever hear, and then encourages them to share that good news with others, who will become their brothers and sisters for eternity. World Impact is a Christian missions organization because as missionaries we minister to the unchurched; we minister cross-culturally; and we establish indigenous churches.

WORLD IMPACT MINISTERS TO THE UNCHURCHED, TO THOSE UNREACHED BY THE GOSPEL

A Christian missionary reaches those who have not heard, *or have not understood,* the gospel. This was Paul's passion: "It has always been my ambition to preach the gospel where Christ was not known so that I would not be building on someone else's foundation. Rather, as it is written: 'Those who were not told about Him will see and those who have not heard will understand'" (Romans 15:20-21).

World Impact targets neighborhoods and ethnic groups which have no easy access to an evangelical church or where large numbers of unreached people need additional churches. Preaching the gospel is the center of all missionary activity (Romans 10:14-15).

The world cannot be won to Christ without reaching the cities:[1] nearly 50% of the world's population lives in cities; the majority are poor and are outside the normal reach of established churches. Few attempts have been made to draw them into congregations.[2]

In the 21st century our globe will have 433 cities which contain over one million people each, while the world's urban population will increase by 1.6 million people per week. As a result, poverty in metropolises will expand, producing a planet of urban slums. To meet these needs, new inner-city churches must be planted on a radically accelerated scale.[3]

WORLD IMPACT MINISTERS CROSS-CULTURALLY

All Christians desire to reach those who have not heard the gospel. However, missionaries reach across cultures and evan-

---

[1]   Ervin E. Hastey, "Reaching the Cities First: A Biblical Model of World Evangelization," *An Urban World: Churches Face the Future,* Larry L. Rose and C. Kirk Hadaway, eds. (Nashville: Broadman Press, 1984), 147.

[2]   Roger S. Greenway and Timothy M. Monsma, *Cities: Mission's New Frontier* (Grand Rapids: Baker, 1989), 169-182.

[3]   Harvie Conn, "Urban Mission," *Toward the 21st Century in Christian Mission,* (Grand Rapids: Eerdmans, 1993), 318-347.

gelize not only individuals, but ethnic and cultural groups.[4] The Book of Acts is the story of cross-cultural evangelism.

America's large cities are increasingly internationalized and ethnically and racially mixed. For example, the United States has the largest African population of every country but Nigeria and the largest Polish population of all nations but Poland. Greater Los Angeles is the second largest Mexican city; New York is the second largest Puerto Rican city. Few evangelical churches exist for many cultural and ethnic groups; some groups have no churches.

Cross-cultural ministry is essential if we are to reach our inner cities for Christ. The key to cross-cultural ministry is building friendships and establishing trust.

Building Cross-Cultural Relationships

For over three decades, thousands of World Impact volunteers and missionaries have ministered among people from different cultures. We have learned many things the hard way. Let me share four crucial steps that facilitate the building of loving relationships.

1. Be A Servant

Jesus, the Church Planter, came humbly. His arrival on earth could have been in a palace, to an emperor, complete with imperial fanfare. He chose rather to be born in a manger to an unwed mother among a conquered people. The One from heaven became Jesus of Nazareth, who eventually gave His life as a ransom for many.

It did not take us long to learn that, like Jesus, we would establish friendships more quickly by serving—playing with a child, painting a room, listening to a concern or just being available in an emergency—than we would by preaching or teaching.

---

[4]   Ralph Winter, "This Highest Priority: Cross-Cultural Evangelism." *Let the Earth Hear His Voice*, (Minneapolis: World Wide Publications, 1975), 221.

Some of our volunteers owned million-dollar businesses, led churches or ran schools, but they built relationships most effectively when they submitted to urban leadership and served in any way they were asked. Submission and servanthood led to trust and facilitated communication.

2. Be Informed

Jesus, the original missionary, was not only painfully aware of man's sinful condition, He became well-versed in the culture into which He was thrust. Jesus listened to, learned from and honored His parents and elders. At the synagogue, He discovered the glory of David and Solomon, and He grieved over the atrocities and captivities inflicted on the Jewish people. He experienced foreign occupation. Before Jesus could be the Jewish Messiah, He had to understand Judaism. For Christ, the culture receiving the gospel took precedence over His own, except where it clearly violated God's law.

Similarly, all Christians need to become informed about the cultures that surround us, especially those cultures among which God calls us to plant churches. A Native American will trust us sooner if we understand Sand Creek and Wounded Knee. A Mexican American will embrace us more quickly if we celebrate Cinco de Mayo together. An African American wants us to understand his history and current condition. We need to know how others feel about the past, and what concerns them now.[5]

Listen To Those Served

Along with serving and staying informed, we need to spend substantially more time listening than talking. "Wise men store up knowledge (they listen), but the mouth of a fool invites ruin" (Proverbs 10:14). If we talk before we listen, we might unintentionally say or do something offensive and strain our relationships.

---

[5] Christian books give us insight and guidance, e.g., *Healing America's Wounds* by John Dawson; *Breaking Down The Walls* by Raleigh Washington and Glen Kehrein; *Let Justice Roll Down* by John Perkins; *More Than Equals* by Spencer Perkins and Chris Rice; *Real Hope in Chicago* by Wayne L. Gordon.

Before we can listen, we must provide a climate where people from other cultures trust us. (That is why serving precedes being informed.) Our new friends will not share what hurts them, nor how they perceive the words and actions of others, if they fear that we will consider them overly sensitive. Let me give you three examples of how I learned by listening.

One. Lauren Gaines, the daughter of evangelist Tom Skinner, recently explained to me how, when she was eight years of age, her grandmother gave her a couple of cotton balls and told Lauren that this was the last cotton she had ever picked. Then Grandma prayed that Lauren would never forget the slavery and cotton picking from which she was spared. Slavery is as close for Americans today as one grandmother-granddaughter chat. Growing up, I used to playfully call friends, "Cotton pickers." I never stopped to think how upsetting and humiliating that would be to my African-American friends like Lauren.

Two. As a child I referred to African Americans as "coons." I now realize that that pejorative nickname came from a game Whites developed to reinforce fear in Blacks. In "coon hunting," a slave was covered with scent and set free to run in the woods at night. Then the slave owners released their hound dogs to track and tree the slaves. Bets were placed on whose dog would catch a slave first. Once caught and treed, the victim was usually shot from the tree like a raccoon. During the early 20th century in Rosewood, Florida a wild game of "coon hunting" lasted for eight days. More than a hundred Blacks were killed.[6]

Three. I recently spent four days in the South with a Christian brother, who shared many insights about the Southern culture. I was ashamed that some Christians continue to celebrate the Confederacy. When an African American sees the Confederate flag honored or hears the band play Dixie he is reminded of slavery, segregation, Jim Crow and discrimination.

A recent presidential candidate, referring to the civil rights marches of the 60's said, "If *they* can sing, 'We Shall Overcome,' *we* can sing 'Dixie.' " I deplore the stated "they-we" division from one who wants to be President of all. And, I am amazed at his callousness. Singing "Dixie" to descendants of slaves would be comparable to singing anthems about Hitler to survivors of the concentration camps.[7]

I always liked "Dixie" until I understood what it meant.

Beware Of Social Snubs

Many ethnic minorities are hurt by social snubs. In the 1990's, Joe Reed, a 23-year-old African-American legislative aide to United States Congressman Earl Hilliard, an Alabama Democrat, was repeatedly stopped by lobbyists sponsoring receptions and asked to produce identification. White aides walked in without interference. Sometimes Joe was turned away and told the gatherings were strictly for members of Congress, but he learned later that that was a lie.

Ken Mulluinex, often the only White among Hilliard's aides attending the receptions, said, "We all go together, and every time they let me walk right in. But Black aides are always stopped and questioned. It happens so many times I can't think it is anything else but a Black-White issue." Reed says, "It makes you feel second-class. No matter how far you go, no matter how well-dressed you are, you are still a nigger before anything else."[8]

Recognize Racial Slights

Most minorities are the brunt of racial slights that are hard to document. A business executive, waiting by the front door of a hotel, was handed a set of car keys and instructed to park a vehicle. Some minorities have been directed by the salesperson to the cheapest suits in a clothing store without being asked; others were refused service in a Denny's restaurant, or required to prepay for the meal; many regularly watch pedestrians speed up, or cross the street, when they see someone from another race approaching. These are but a small sample of what millions of Americans experience every day.

---

[7]   *U.S. News and World Report* (July 15, 1996), 76.

[8]   "Social Snubs Still Hurt Blacks Despite Rights' Gains," *Newark Star Ledger,* n.d.

Even well-meaning Christians who visit our ministry have hurt our staff and neighbors. Let me give you a few examples of what believers have said:

- "Aren't you afraid your (White staff) children will be corrupted by the children in the city?"
- "All Blacks look alike. I cannot tell one child from another."
- "You cannot trust those (Mexicans, Blacks, Hmong, etc)."
- "Parents can't even spell their kids' names right." (Names are sometimes spelled differently from how they sound).
- A Bible-club volunteer's low expectations: "I let the children run wild. I understand the bad homes they have come from."
- "Willie is such a little monkey" (This offends people whose race has been unjustly characterized as primate.)

This damage is tragic because the visitor genuinely wants to be part of building the Church but unknowingly is insensitive to the receiving culture.

Honor The Poor

The American Church unconsciously discriminates against the poor. A recent spiritual warfare conference cost $250 per participant. I asked for scholarships for some potential delegates. The best deal I could get was 50% off, which was still too expensive for the poor. The conference would have helped our neighbors but was inaccessible.

The poor cannot afford many Christian concerts, spiritual gatherings or prayer breakfasts, unless they are connected to "worthy" organizations. The poor seldom have credit cards to reserve seats or order curriculum over the phone. There *is* a class division in the Church.

We need to *ask God to make us sensitive* to racial, cultural or class discrimination, bias or slights. We need to refuse to be a part of them and then vigorously stand against them. This will demonstrate our love for the poor and the "outsider."

Learn From The Community

Every culture has unique rituals and customs that an outsider would never know if someone did not teach him. A friend of mine who went to Tibet with a group of Christians provides a classic example. They were warned not to touch anything in homes they entered because the residents, out of Christian love, would give the visitors everything they touched, even though the Tibetans could not afford to lose the objects. One visitor either did not hear the instruction, or he forgot it. Trying to be complimentary, he raved about and touched several items in the home. These were then given to the culturally-forgetful visitor as he was leaving.

The guide insisted that the guest take everything given to him or the owners would be deeply insulted, feeling that the visitor did not think their gifts were good enough for him. How much more compassionate the visitor would have been had he heeded the cultural mores! We must be informed.

3. Recognize Sins And Repent

When we ask God to make us sensitive to cross-cultural issues, He will convict us through His Holy Spirit and scripture. As we learn about the hurt and pain that have been caused by our actions—that off-color joke about a cotton picker, a coon, a wetback, an Indian; or that subtle prejudice, "Some homeless Black guy must have done it"—even if we meant no harm, we need to be willing to repent for the bitterness and brokenness we have caused.

I grew up in Portland, Oregon, the son of a Youth for Christ director. As a child, I accompanied Christian teenagers who were going to Winona Lake, Indiana to compete in Youth For Christ preaching, singing and Bible-quiz competitions. On one such trip, we were not permitted to eat in a restaurant because we had Black teenagers with us. My father was indignant. I do not remember the outcome, but I did know something was wrong when teenagers were humiliated because of the shade of their skin.

Another thing was wrong. The fact that I was so surprised by a restaurant's treatment of Blacks illustrated how isolated I was. In reflection, I had no Black friends. I had grown up in a Christian world, but in a *segregated* Christian world—far from God's inclusive standard.

Racism subtly reared its ugly head throughout my early years. In fourth grade, our neighborhood was up in arms, fearing a dramatic drop in real estate values because a Chinese doctor was going to move in. Scores of Mexican Americans attended the same high school I attended for four years. Yet I do not think I ever met, or even knew the name of, one Hispanic teenager. I never realized I was as racially isolated as pre-Cornelius Peter. However, racial and cultural comfort zones must not stand in the way of Christ's all inclusive, reconciling work through me, and they should not for the Church either.

Many Christians need to repent of racism. Prejudice can be as addictive as heroin. It can habitually spew out of our mouths with no thought about how it hurts our brothers or sisters, or their Father. God forbid that we drive one person away from the Church because of a hint of prejudice. Lord, convict us and heal us of our sin.

What if God called me to minister in My Lai, the scene of America's 1968 massacre of more than 300 unarmed Vietnamese civilians?[9] Before I could build friendships with the children of the victims, I would have to know what happened, listen to how the children felt and take responsibility for the sins of my countrymen, even though I never personally took part in My Lai. I would have to apologize on behalf of my nation, with whom the Vietnamese would associate me.

I could reason that the American infantry had been bitterly contesting this Viet Cong stronghold and anticipated a violent engagement. I could argue that civilians in My Lai had killed Americans. *But that is not the point.*

Jesus could have righteously damned the human race, but He came with a towel and a cross. If we are going to plant

---

[9]   On March 16, 1968, an American infantry company herded women, children and old men into ditches and shot them. Grollier Electronic Publishing, 1995.

churches among the urban poor, we must come as servants. Then we can earn the right to be heard.

As a member of the dominant culture, my sin has most often been silence. When a taxi passes by an African-American brother and picks me up instead—or when I am served before an Hispanic in a restaurant or a store—too often I have been quiet. My sins have been unperceived racism—locking the door of my car when I see a big man of color standing on the corner on a dark night. I have been insensitive to the pain of others, often out of ignorance. Of these sins, I repent. I ask God and my sisters and brothers, "Forgive me."

4. Respect Each Other

A gaping racial division surfaced after the announcement of the O.J. Simpson verdict in 1995. Most African Americans were pleased, while many White Americans stood in complete dismay. My wife was with a group of Christian women when the verdict was announced. An African-American sister whispered, "I knew he was innocent." An Anglo sister was dumbfounded.

How could Christian women, who love the same Lord, view the same verdict so differently?

My index finger illustrates how these diverse opinions could occur. When the index finger on my left hand is directly in front of my nose, the nail is on the left side of that finger. Expert witnesses, or random observers, can affirm that fact. However, if you stand in front of me, on the other side of my left finger facing me, you might say that the nail was on the right-hand side of the finger.

Both of us are looking at the same nail on the same finger at the same time. However, reality appears different depending upon our point of view. To disagree with someone's perspective does not mean that their view is invalid.

For alienation to end, we need to understand people from different cultures. We must listen to them, communicate with them and perhaps, even walk to the other side of the finger. We may not always agree, but we can respect their perspective.

The best way for me to be your friend is to serve you, to listen to you, to confess and repent if I hurt you, and to respect and love you, *no strings attached.* Relationships occur over a period of time, not in one or two visits. Friendships are essential for effective cross-cultural ministry: this is the gate through which we must pass to obey the Great Commission and make disciples of all people groups.

WORLD IMPACT ESTABLISHES INDIGENOUS, CULTURALLY-CONDUCIVE CHURCHES

The Church's early missionaries always did more than make converts across culture; they made disciples, who become leaders of local congregations (Acts 18:11; 20:17-38; I Timothy 3:1-13; II Timothy 2:2). The missionaries then moved on to new areas to repeat the process.

Following this model, World Impact evangelizes those who are unchurched in the inner city and plants evangelical churches[10] where new believers can experience Christ and mature in their faith within their own culture. As these churches become self-sufficient, we expect them to take responsibility for evangelizing their neighbors and reproducing new churches. World Impact then continues in our missionary task of bringing the gospel to other cultural groups who have not yet heard of Christ, or accepted Him (I Corinthians 9:19-23).

Church planting does not involve "sheep stealing." We do *not* want to attract believers from other community churches who might come because they like our preaching, teaching or worship. Our desire is to reach the unchurched, those who have never heard or understood the gospel of Jesus.

---

[10] There is only <u>one</u> Church. Christ is its head and all Christians are its members. Members commit to knowing Christ (being made perfect and complete in Him) and making Him known (being used by the Holy Spirit to fulfill Christ's commission in the world). They gather regularly in Christ's name to honor and glorify God and delight in Him through corporate worship and to participate in the sacraments. They are subject to Christ's authority and lordship as revealed in the Holy Scriptures, taught by the Holy Spirit and exercised by His appointed leaders. They encourage a biblical lifestyle. They confront broken relationships and oppression wherever they find it.

More Churches Needed

Some people ask, "Don't we have enough churches already?" The answer is, "No!" For example, metropolitan Los Angeles has ten million people[11] of which *eight million* are unchurched. If we planted 100 churches for each of the next 25 years (2500 churches) and each church grew to 200 members (the average church in America has around 100 members) we would have reached 500,000 people, leaving seven and one-half million unchurched.

We will not have enough churches until every person is in one. We encourage all evangelical churches to join with us in a massive cross-cultural church-planting effort among the urban poor. We do this for eight reasons:

1. *God commands it*. He instructed us to build His Church. It is our privilege to help Him prepare His Bride for the wedding feast of the Lamb (Revelations 19:9).

2. *The model of the early Church*. The new Church in Antioch sent missionary teams to evangelize those who had never heard. When the Christian faith expanded, it spread in churches. Each new church is responsible for planting another.

3. *Churches conserve fruit*. Jesus wants new believers to be grounded (John 15:16) and to mature in their faith (Hebrews 12:1-3). Without the accountability and nurture of other Christians, new believers tend to remain weak or wither in their faith and stumble in their walk with God.

4. *Society is changed*. Christians promote righteousness, peace and justice. They strive to overcome bitterness, prejudice, racism, hate and injustice.

5. *The Church stimulates healing*. Reconciliation with God and man is the reason behind, and the by-product of, church planting (Psalm 133:1).

6. *The Great Commission requires it*. The greatest numbers of unreached people are among the urban poor. They are growing more rapidly than the rest of society. Church planting is part of God's method to gather and preserve the harvest.

[11] 1990 figures, David Barrett, *World-Class Cities and World Evangelization*, (Birmingham, AL: New Hope, 1986), p.49.

7. _Not all church plants will succeed._

8. _Demographics change._ The constant cultural ebb and flow of city neighborhoods often makes existing churches less effective than they once were and creates opportunities for new church plants.

If every missions agency were to invest their time, energy and money in planting churches in Los Angeles, it would be easier and less expensive than sending people to the four corners of the earth: if churches were planted among each of the 157 major people groups in Los Angeles, we would have first-generation links with 98% of the population of the planet.

Disciples from these newly-planted churches could be commissioned to declare the gospel in their country of origin. They are already fluent in their native language, culturally sensitive and indigenously connected. An explosion of diverse Christian churches in America's cities would impact the entire world.[12]

Many United States cities are similar demographically to Los Angeles. "Minorities now account for more than half the population in many of the nation's largest cities."[13] We need to gear up now for the influx of urban poor in the next few years or the numbers will be overwhelming.

Summary

World Impact is a Christian missions organization, whose ministry focuses on America's urban poor, but whose vision is to make disciples of all peoples worldwide.

1. World Impact ministers to the unchurched.
2. World Impact ministers cross-culturally.
3. World Impact establishes indigenous, culturally-conducive churches.

---

[12] This is not intended to discount the value of foreign missions. It is only a suggestion of an additional strategy to reach the world for Christ.

[13] William P. O'Hare, "America's Minorities–The Demographics of Diversity," _Population Bulletin_, Vol. 47, No. 4., Mary Mederios Kent, ed. (Washington, D.C.: December, 1992), 23.

SECTION IV
A GLIMPSE OF BEAUTY: HOPE!

"Why are you downcast, O my soul? Why so disturbed within me? Put your hope in God" (Psalm 42:5).

For over two decades I have watched God use World Impact missionaries to touch thousands of individuals and families with the gospel. Yet I must confess that when the 1992 riots surfaced the underlying alienation, I wondered again, "Can God even heal this city?"

That is when Isaiah's words spoke to me, "But those who hope in the Lord will renew their strength. They will soar on wings like eagles; they will run and not grow weary, they will walk and not be faint" (Isaiah 40:31).

God has restored my hope that He wants, and is able, to save not just a remnant, but the majority of people in our urban centers. This section shares that good news of hope.

Chapter XIII

Against All Odds:
The Early Church

The Church of Jesus Christ offers the hope, the antidote to alienation, that the urban poor seek. However, churches have historically flourished in homogeneous societies, where everyone looked alike, spoke the same language, shared similar customs and history, and maintained reasonably cohesive communities. Look around next Sunday and see if this describes your place of worship.

When missionaries go to a foreign land, their hearers usually live in an homogeneous community. For example, before learning about Jesus, residents in a Filipino village would already share a common tradition and similar customs, and they would all speak Tagalog.

But our inner cities are racially and culturally diverse, economically depressed, alienated from other classes as well as estranged from God. Are the entanglements of conflicting customs and languages, age-long prejudices and habitual racism so squelching that God Himself is frustrated at bringing harmony out of this boiling pot? Can even the Lord alleviate the hopelessness of the city?

Should we Christians throw up our hands and admit that we do not have an adequate response to the desperation of the urban poor? Has there ever been a multicultural, racially-diverse society like this, where the church has flourished and spread?

Yes. At least one—first century Rome.

A Model Of Diversity

Early believers faced challenges similar to ours in the Roman Empire. A mixture of nationalities, languages, cultures, races, ethnic groups and religions caused divisions in society and alienation among people, comparable to those presently occurring in our cities.

Rome, too, was a society of haves and have nots. Rome dominated commerce, wealth and economic power in the world. Its military-industrial complex and trade network supported the Roman armies in the provinces and the vast bureaucracy that managed the empire.

Rome had slaves, former slaves, foreigners and disenfranchised poor, who were often exploited in their occupations, unemployed or living on the dole.[1] Immigrants from all parts of the empire crowded into urban centers hoping to escape poverty, seeking social or economic betterment or succumbing to the fascination of the great cities. Many were not citizens.

The Apostle Paul probably lived in Subura, an urban slum of Rome marked by narrow streets, open sewers, poor housing, crowded conditions and intense interaction. Nero likely burned Rome to clear out this impoverished section, not expecting the fire to get out of hand.[2]

These problems seemed politically and economically unsolvable. But instead of resigning themselves to defeat, Christians capitalized on the opportunities. Emerging churches became responsible alternatives for Romans who were seeking spiritual fulfillment. Christian bodies offered fresh beliefs and values, and a unique lifestyle of community, as they do to inner-city residents today. Now, as then, the Church provides a long-term solution to a world at war with itself and alienated from God for four key reasons:

1. The Church was sensitive to the poor and oppressed. It fed and cared for the widows and orphans and gave money to

---

[1] The infamous "bread and circus" for the urban poor. "Rome (Italy)," *Microsoft Encarta.* Copyright ©1993 Microsoft Corporation. Copyright ©1993 Funk and Wagnall's Corporation.

[2] Joseph P. Fitzpatrick, *Paul: Saint of The Inner City* (New York: Paulist Press, 1990), 75-76.

struggling congregations. It understood that Jesus healed the sick, made the blind to see, the deaf to hear and the lame to walk, but that He never performed a *deed* of the Kingdom without declaring a *word* of the Kingdom. Service always grew out of evangelism, discipleship and establishing new churches.

Christian compassion drove Paul to look past the immense problems of the urban poor and to see their potential as followers of God who would be transformed into His Bride. The Lord told Paul, "I have a great following in (Corinth)" (Acts 18:10), a place where most Christians would have given up. Believing and seeing the best in people is nothing new for the company of the committed.

2. The Church had the potential for dynamic growth and revival as God's Spirit responded to the repentance, prayers and service of His people. It started with a small band of believers, but spread all across North Africa, Asia Minor and Europe.

3. The Church crossed class and cultural lines.[3] The multiethnic Church pulled together people from every culture, race, gender and class into a common community. A homogeneous Church would not have challenged the root problems of Roman fragmentation.

4. The Church focused on people's primary need, healing their estrangement from God. The only remedy to the hopelessness of the urban poor was for them to be united with God through Christ.

And so, reconciliation to God and to one another, which started small as a mustard seed, flourished as the gospel was declared and demonstrated. The message and ministry of the Church combined evangelism with practical expressions of love for a lost and broken world (Acts 2:42-47; 4:32-36).

The Source Of Hope

Today, as in the ancient world, only the Church can transform alienation into salvation and despair into hope for the urban

---

[3] Kenneth Scott Latourette, *A History of Christianity, Volume 1: Beginnings to 1500* (New York: Harper-Row, 1975), 106.

poor. "Christ in you, the hope of glory" (Colossians 1:27). The urban poor are important to God (James 2) and are to be treated like Christ Himself (Matthew 25). They also wait for the blessed hope, the glorious appearing of our great God and Savior, Jesus Christ (Titus 2:13).

The 1992 riots would have been far worse had the Church been entirely absent from the city. Pastors and parishioners calmed the young and defended the helpless. *While the government was debating a response, the Church was in the streets with food, brooms, hugs and assurance.* But since less than 10% of the urban poor attend church, the impact, while important, was not widespread.

A New Explosion

Since the 1992 riots, inner-city Christians have been calling for an equally spontaneous, but far more constructive, explosion initiated by God and nurtured by His Holy Spirit. It will transform death into life and despair into hope. During the riots, so many fires were lit simultaneously that for every blaze extinguished, three or four more exploded in widely-scattered neighborhoods.

Fire symbolizes God's presence in the burning bush (Exodus 3:2), in the pillar that guided the children of Israel out of captivity (Exodus 13:21), at Mt. Sinai (Exodus 19:18) and at Pentecost (Acts 2:3). Like Israel we pray for God's deliverance, guidance and power.

We seek to proliferate God's presence in the city, praying for thousands of spiritual fires to be lit (churches planted) among the urban poor in hundreds of neighborhoods with millions of people—so many that the devil and all his legions will not be able to extinguish them.

We believe these churches will spread like a 100-mile-per-hour firestorm, winning the lost and freeing the captives, and that the gates of hell will not be able to withstand this holy conflagration (Matthew 16:18). The Church of Jesus Christ will triumph!

Chapter XIV

If They Can Do It:
Our Historical Model[1]

Is it reasonable to believe that thousands of churches can be planted among the urban poor? Many Americans sincerely question whether the poor can be empowered to do anything for themselves, let alone for Christ; others wonder if the poor must always depend upon the dominant culture for money, leadership and other resources.

A First-Century Firestorm

The first-century Church provides us with hope. It spread like wildfire among the poor and oppressed of the Roman Empire to the boundaries of the then-known world. Those new believers had few physical resources and faced ominous threats, yet they established thousands of gatherings of committed disciples of Christ.

I used to accept the feats of early Christians nonchalantly. I skimmed over their stories without thinking about what they actually did or the obstacles they really faced. Maybe I was reading the New Testament as a novel instead of as an eyewitness account of ordinary people empowered by the living God. But recently, the Lord showed me that the Book of Acts is about

---

[1] Don Davis and Terry Cornett "Working the Vision: Toward a Theology of the Church: Drafting a Vision of Winning Our Cities for Christ" (Los Angeles: World Impact Press, 1996).

obedient people in *my* world. Their principles of ministry are transferable to our inner cities.

Think about the expansion of the early Church. Imagine a rugged Jewish fisherman physically embracing Cornelius, a Gentile. Capture Peter's fear, questions, expectations, surprise and exhilaration as he participated in Christianity's jump of a seemingly unscalable cultural hurdle.

Reflect on Saul, the scholarly pharisee who had the ancient equivalent of a Th.D and a Ph.D., being blinded by God's glory and supernaturally transformed into Paul. This Jew among Jews launched out to plant churches among infidels!

Envision Paul, arriving at Corinth, being greeted at the city gates by temple prostitutes offering him a diversion from his weariness. Brazen signs pointed to brothels, vomitoriums and every other immorality imaginable.

In the midst of this hedonism, materialism and idolatry, Paul preached about a holy God and the resurrection of Jesus Christ. What are the odds of people believing (the first time they heard) that Jesus lived a perfect life, died to pay for their sins and rose from the dead? Paul's listeners had never heard of Jesus. They did not have CNN, books or newspapers to document Christ's virgin birth or resurrection, or even the claims of His Incarnation or empty tomb. And Nazareth—could anything good come from there?

If a person walked into your home today and said a holy man had been born of a virgin, had lived a sinless life, was crucified, buried, and then three days later burst out of his tomb, would you even investigate? Or would you just call 9-1-1 and try to have the messenger committed?

Amazingly, due to the preaching of the Word of God (Jesus) and the power of the Holy Spirit, Corinthians believed Paul's reasoned arguments based upon Jewish scripture, repented of their sins and became Christians! Praise God for this miraculous evangelism! It gives us hope and inspiration.

Who were these new believers? Celcus, the second-century pagan author of a trenchant attack on Christianity, accused

Christians of "...deliberately excluding educated people by re-
cruiting the ignorant, foolish, dishonorable, stupid, slaves,
women and little children. Christian evangelists were wool-
workers, cobblers and laundry-workers. Jesus had only been able
to win disciples among tax collectors and sailors, people who
had not even a primary education."[2]

How could Paul plant a church among these economically-
deprived, theological neophytes? He had no New Testament,
theological books or tracts to give them. They had no access to
Christian television, video teachings, radio or seminaries.

But something amazing happened. Paul spent between five
and eighteen months in each city,[3] appointed believers who felt
responsible to evangelize and nurture new converts in their communities, and left.

The outcome? Most would have predicted few lasting conversions and a short-lived Church after Paul's departure. But
something supernatural happened. These novitiates gathered to
worship God, ignoring former racial, cultural, social and economic barriers. In Christ, they were one. He was in them, and
they were in Him! When churches were born, they multiplied
so fast that historians would have needed a computer to keep
up with their proliferation.

These new congregations had no cathedrals of their own.
They gathered in homes, cemeteries or parks. Believers had no
time to construct sanctuaries—they were too busy building the
Church. Only after Constantine legitimized Christianity and
erected cathedrals around the shrines of martyrs did Christians
forget that they *are* the Church and start to think about *going* to
church.[4]

The irresistible expansion of the Christian faith during its
first 120 years reflected its physical and social personal mobil-

---

2   Wayne A. Meeks *The First Urban Christians: The Social World of the Apostle Paul*
    (New Haven: Yale University Press, 1983) 51.
3   Roland Allen, *Missionary Methods: St. Paul's or Ours?* (Grand Rapids: Eerdmans,
    1962) 84-85.
4   John McManners, ed., *The Oxford Illustrated History of Christianity* (Oxford: Oxford
    University Press, 1990), 80.

ity.[5] Wherever Christians went—to a new city, a different job or another neighborhood—they took Christ with them and planted churches. The only plausible explanation for the exponential explosion of the Church was that Christians experienced a mighty moving of the Holy Spirit.

Since the gospel transformed the splintered, multicultural, racially-and socially-divided Roman world, it can heal our inner cities. Let's examine two facts:

The Early Church Grew With Few Physical Resources

1. A small work force. Paul was often alone, or worked with one or two brothers and sisters (Philippians 2:19-24). Once he said, "No one came to my support, but everyone deserted me" (II Timothy 4:16-18). The harvest was plentiful, but the laborers were few.

2. Poor transportation. Paul walked for days over dusty roads and rugged trails that would have physically deterred most people. He sailed on ships that ran aground and broke into pieces (Acts 27:41). He did not even have a car that could have been stolen, burned, vandalized or broken down; let alone buses, trains or planes.

3. Little financial backing. Paul said, "To this very hour, we go hungry and thirsty, we are in rags, we are brutally treated, we are homeless. We work hard with our own hands. We have become the scum of the earth, the refuse of the world" (I Corinthians 4:11-13).

4. No seminaries or publishing houses. Paul asked the Colossians to read his letter and then send it on to the Laodiceans (Colossians 4:16). He had no photocopy machines. His curriculum did not relate to Gentiles in the city. The material available (the Septuagint) was in the wrong language, written from a different cultural perspective, too bulky to carry in a pocket and extremely difficult for most new converts to understand.

---

[5] Meeks, 17.

5. Primitive communication. When Paul wanted to find out how things were going in a church he had planted he could not telephone, fax, e-mail or tune in to the Trinity Broadcasting Network. He had to send one of his disciples, who traveled weeks or months, to communicate with the newly-planted churches (I Thessalonians 3:1-5; Colossians 4:16).

The limited physical resources of the early Church should answer any questions about God's ability to plant churches among the poor in America. The unemployed, widows, orphans—even slaves—can tithe, support a pastor and share Christ with others. You cannot out-give God. Churches are being planted in poverty-stricken third world cities, among squatters and in jails!

The Early Church Grew In Spite Of Facing Ominous Threats

1. They faced persecution from Judaism, a "sister" religion (Acts 9:23-25). Some Jews swore not to eat or drink until they had killed Paul (Acts 23:12). They tried to influence Festus to transfer Paul to Jerusalem so that they could kill him along the way (Acts 25:3). Many Christians were impaled, doused with oil and lit on fire to provide light.
2. They fought discouragement. Paul says, "I have worked much harder, been in prison more frequently, been flogged more severely and been exposed to death again and again. Five times I received from the Jews the forty lashes minus one. Three times I was beaten with rods, once I was stoned, three times I was shipwrecked...I have gone without sleep; I have been cold and naked. Besides everything else, I face daily the pressure of my concern for all the churches" (II Corinthians 11:23-28).
3. They were confronted with idols (Acts 17:16; 19:23 ff.), immorality (1 Peter 4:3-6) and bizarre philosophies like the New Moon celebration and the worship of angels (Colossians 2:16-23).

4. Their leaders were intimidated. Peter was jailed for preaching (Acts 5:17ff.). Stephen was stoned (Acts 7:54ff.); James, the brother of John, was killed with a sword (Acts 12:1ff.) and all of the Apostles, except John, were martyred.

5. They experienced rivalry among some of their converts (I Corinthians 3:1-4). The Corinthians acted like the theological forerunners of the Bloods and the Crips.

6. They had a legacy of racial, cultural and class hatred (Romans 10-11), the roots of which ran far deeper than any in our present day (Ephesians 2).

7. They had workers, converted from pagan religions, who were former idolaters, adulterers, male prostitutes, homosexuals, thieves, drunks and slanderers (I Corinthians 6:9-11).

Why The Early Church Grew So Rapidly

Paul had few advantages over present-day missionaries.[6] The early Church used the same resources available to us—God's Word and His Spirit—to face similar cultural, social-class and moral barriers.

When God calls people to advance His Kingdom in a missionary enterprise, He enables them to carry out His instruction. The Holy Spirit selects missionary teams (Acts 13:2) and endows them with gifts to enhance the Church numerically and spiritually (I Corinthians 12).

The Holy Spirit taught early Christians (John 15:26), guided them in the truth (John 16:13), filled them with strength (Acts 2:4), confirmed the preaching of God's Word with miracles and signs of God's Kingdom and empowered them to be witnesses of Christ (Acts 1:8). He directed the affairs of the Church (Acts 15:28), enabled believers to minister boldly in Christ's name (Acts 4:13), appointed overseers to shepherd God's people (Acts 20:28) and increased the effectiveness of prayer (Romans 8:26).

---

[6] Ronald Allen, *Missionary Methods: St. Paul's or Ours?* (Grand Rapids, MI: Wm. B. Eerdmans Publishing Co., 1962), 1-95.

Men and women who are called by God (Galatians 1:10-11), are available to Him (I Corinthians 9:15-23), rely on His wisdom and resources (Philippians 3:4-16) and trust His provision through His indwelling Spirit (II Corinthians 1:18-22) can plant churches among the urban poor. It is no more difficult today than it was in the first century.

Nor is it any easier. Jesus calls His disciples to take up their cross and follow Him. They have to die to themselves, give God all that they have, and pour out their lives for others. But Christians who submit to God's call will be blessed like Peter, Paul and Philip, who carried the good news to those who had not heard nor understood the gospel.

Chapter XV

We Can Do It:
Reaching The Unchurched

Planting churches is the only way to transform alienation into hope, and chaos into peace. It was true in the first century, and it is true today. If ever there were people who deserved the nurture, love, protection and affirmation of the Church, it is the urban poor. The Church is one institution that the poor can run themselves—without government, or monied and influential people calling the shots. The Church empowers the poor.

The Conviction: Promote Independence

As our understanding of empowering the urban poor increased, our attention focused more on church planting. We always knew our neighbors should be churched. It now became evident that for lasting change to occur, it had to be *our neighbors'* church.

We discovered that we should be planting indigenous churches rather than "conducting church" for new believers. Consequently, we decided to transform our "Celebration" service (see page 96) from a staff-led and staff-attended church into a self-sufficient, community-led congregation. After much prayer and waiting on the Lord, Fred Stoesz, a World Impact career missionary, became our lead church planter in Los Angeles.

131

Initially, we released as many missionaries as possible from their leadership involvement in Celebration. We asked several other missionaries to worship elsewhere so that they would not dominate the Celebration Church simply by their presence. This church growth in reverse left some gaping holes in what the people attending had come to expect. For example, the music was suddenly scaled down from a large worship team to Fred playing the piano with one finger!

Although the changes startled many, in a short time, God honored our decisions by inspiring community residents to assume leadership. Several people had not led previously because, in our zeal to *serve* them, we had not left them any opportunity to *lead*. But there were emerging leaders. We commissioned a church-planting team consisting of five World Impact missionaries and three community families:

Ron Johnson, Virgil Gray's brother, had realized his goal of escaping the inner city by purchasing a house in the suburbs. However, the Lord called Ron, his wife, Louise, and their three children back to South Central to minister.

Luis Perez had grown up in Guatemala. After marrying Sonia and fathering two children, Luis' alcohol abuse led to a separation. After he reunited with his family in Los Angeles, World Impact missionaries invited the Perez children to Bible club. Luis soon accepted Christ, joined a weekly men's study, and before long was leading a Spanish-speaking Sunday school class in the Celebration Church.

Enrique Santis grew up with a Christian mother in Guatemala. From age 14 to 18, he helped his pastor evangelize and plant five churches in Guatemalan villages. After coming to Los Angeles, Enrique met and married Silvia, who had come to Los Angeles from El Salvador.

Dynamic Team Work

God uses teams to plant vibrant churches. Jesus formed a team and He sent out His disciples in pairs (Mark 6:7; Luke 10:1). Peter and John formed the Hebraic team (Galatians 2:1-

11); Paul formed the Gentile team (Acts 13:1-3);[1] Paul even had a "prison" team (II Timothy 4:9-13)—the original "cell" church.

God promises, "Five of you will chase a hundred, and a hundred of you will chase ten thousand, and your enemies will fall by the sword before you" (Leviticus 26:8). God multiplies human effort when people work together. "Two are better than one...a cord of three strands is not quickly broken" (Ecclesiastes 4:9-12). A team has exponential power. One horse can pull two tons; two horses working together can pull 23 tons.[2]

Demonstrating The Declared

The team's life together demonstrated the gospel that they declared. Fred's respectful treatment of Ron, Enrique and Luis communicated the biblical truth, "love your neighbor," better than Fred's preaching.

Team members supported each other during times of persecution, loneliness and isolation (II Timothy 4:9-13). They used their unique gifts to work toward the common good of the Kingdom. The team's unity, even when they disagreed, caused people to believe in Christ (John 17:22-23).

The team exemplified the forgiveness, reconciliation and harmony of the Christian community that it desired to create before the eyes of the emerging church: the Celebration Christian Church-planting team was led by a Mennonite missionary from Canada; other members came from Kansas, California, Guatemala and El Salvador.[3] Kingdom life was embodied within the team (John 13:35) as well as proclaimed by the team.

---

[1] Paul mentions 38 partners in ministry. David W. Shenk and Ervin R. Stutzman, *Creating Communities of the Kingdom: New Testament Models of Church Planting* (Scottdale, PA: Herald Press, 1988), 49.

Shenk and Stutzman, 50.

[3] Paul's third missionary journey included Tychichus and Trophinus, Gentiles from Ephesus in the Roman province of Asia; Timothy, an Asian Jew from the Roman province of Galatia; Aristarchus and Gaius, Macedonian Gentiles; Sopater, a Macedonian Jew; and Secundus, a Gentile. His name "second" indicates he was a slave, or former slave.

Leadership Training

There are two basic types of church planters: "Fluid, missionary church planters," whose aim is to train leaders to teach others; and "structural church planters," whose goal is to evangelize and lead new converts themselves.[4] Let me explain the difference. If I lead Raul to the Lord, he would be excited about his new-found faith, deliverance from bondage and relationship with Christ.

A few days later, Raul says, "Keith, Christ did great things for me. But if you think I needed Jesus, you should meet Hector, my cousin. He gambles, beats his wife and smokes dope. Will you tell Hector about Jesus?"

Keith, the structural church planter, almost knocks Raul over to get to Hector. However, Keith, the fluid church planter, would respond, "No, but I will go with you, Raul, as *you* tell Hector." Raul knows nearly nothing about the Bible. However, there is one scriptural principle he knows well enough to communicate, the principle of salvation by faith alone.

So Raul shares Jesus with Hector, who also accepts Christ. Then, when Hector has a question, whom does he call? Keith (the church planter)? Of course, not. He asks Raul.

But Raul does not even know where the Book of Acts is yet—so Raul asks me. Now I have a captive audience, Raul, eager to learn God's Word and motivated by his desire and opportunity to teach Hector. Within one week, indigenous leadership is being developed.

---

[4] Both church-planting strategies have multiple variations:

1. "Fluid, missionary church planting" begins with a team who understand that they will *not* be the future leaders; they will *not* pastor, nor continue as elders, any longer than needed. Their priority is to train and disciple *leaders*.

2. "Structural church planting" begins with a small team of church planters who have decided *they* will be the future leaders of the church they plant. *They* will pastor and set the tone of the new church. They will be the leaders and will disciple *members*.

Each approach is good and necessary. Structural church planting combines formal education and a series of qualifiers for a candidate to be ordained. Fluid, missionary church planting is quicker and emphasizes learning by doing, along with theological education at the church or simultaneous with ministry. The fluid, missionary church planter produces new churches quickly and holds high promise for the dramatic transformation of America's inner cities.

Raul might become the first pastor; Hector, an elder. Both will naturally continue to share their faith with friends and relatives, and the Church will grow. We follow Christ's method of teaching by doing, accompanied by explanation and commentary. Eventually, more and more of the leadership will be passed to Raul, Hector and to those whom they lead to Christ.

Like Paul, who equipped leaders quickly, Fred, as a church planter, wanted to prepare the three indigenous men on his team to lead the church.[5] Sharing responsibility and power makes it easier to include indigenous converts of the newly-planted church in leadership, and provides safety through the counsel of many (Proverbs 13:20). Team members learn from each other and teach one another. Iron sharpens iron (Proverbs 27:17), leading to effective disciple-making.

A community advisory council at Celebration Christian Church helped lead and discern God's direction for "their church." English- and Spanish-speaking congregations were established in the church. They enjoyed bilingual praise and worship, communion, baptisms and feasts and festivals together, but met separately for teaching and some prayer meetings to allow individuals the comfort of their heart language.

In 1993, the church appointed elders and deacons and began training them. Training pastors, leaders and members is an ongoing process that starts with the missionary and continues with the pastors throughout the life of the church. While anxious to multiply, we want to reproduce truth. World Impact is committed to training urban Christians. (See *Addendum D*, The Urban Institute).[6]

Soon Fred had equipped his three "interns" so well that he could cease his "upfront" leadership of the church. Fred's training of leaders culminated when the church called Ron and Luis to pastor the two congregations. Fred and Enrique were then free

---

[5] A church that sends its pastors and elders elsewhere to get training to lead and disciple its people usually does not multiply rapidly. Samuel M. James, "Training for Urban Evangelization," *An Urban World*, Larry Rose and C. Kirk Hadaway, eds (Nashville: Broadman, 1984), 200-201.

[6] The Urban Institute, World Impact's training arm, brings ongoing theological training to inner-city pastors and lay people.

to plant new churches in other communities.

Released For Growth

While the Celebration Christian Church was growing, World Impact sought to empower it, without interfering with its authority. The church used THE OAKS, our camp and retreat center, and church members' children had priority in admission to our school.

However, this dynamic young congregation took responsibility for their pastors' salaries, established their own offices and began paying rent for the use of our facilities. Churches that cannot support a pastor seldom plant a church for others.

The Celebration Christian Church had become healthy when they thought of the Lord as theirs, not a God belonging to "others;" when they met cultural needs around them; when they worshiped in patterns they understood; and when they participated in a body which looked, sounded and functioned as part of the indigenous culture.[7]

A key principle in missionary church planting among the urban poor is, "If what the missionary does cannot be quickly imitated by others, do not do it." The dominant culture tends to view the poor as needy objects of ministry incapable of becoming independent or self-sustaining, unable to generate their own leadership. But the Church *empowers* the poor. We must not foster dependence at the expense of maturity.

Even well-intentioned dependence destroys dynamism and slows growth. Just as it is inappropriate to hand feed and dress a healthy teenager, it is stifling not to encourage independence in each church plant as soon as possible. We must use our resources wisely. Encouraging new churches to become independent is essential if they are to reproduce additional churches.[8]

---

[7] Allan Tippet, *Introduction to Missiology* (Pasadena, CA: William Carey Library, 1987) 381.

[8] At first the relationship between the church planter and the church is highly dependent. As the process develops, less dependence follows, leading to mature independence, which is actually interdependence. Every member of Christ's body depends on the other, or there is alienation and hopelessness.

Partners In Building The Kingdom

Responsible independence does not mean isolation. It means interdependence. When a child matures, she no longer relies on her parents for her daily provisions. She then relates to them more as peers—she enjoys their company, seeks their wisdom and honors their input into her life. But she is responsible for her daily needs and well-being, for nurturing her children and for developing intimate relationships with her friends.

Once a church is birthed, the church planters encourage the new believers to be responsible for their spiritual and financial well-being. One sign of maturity is the new church's recognition that it cannot exist in isolation. It will associate with other newly-planted churches, church associations or denominations to receive input, accountability, instruction and fellowship. But each individual church, not World Impact, will decide with whom it associates.

This maturing process is illustrated in the following graph prepared by our Vice President of Ministries, Dr. David Klopfenstein.

The Maturing Process
Of Indigenous Churches

Qualities Of Young Churches		Qualities Of Maturing Churches
Narrow Interests		Broad Interests
Limited Abilities	The Maturing Church	Large Abilities
Ethnocentric		Inclusive Of Other Ethnic Groups
Passivity Towards Multiculturalism	Newly-Formed Church Plant	Active Concern For Other Cultures
Dependence		Autonomy

Transformation And Growth

A (Depedent)   **Z** (Independent)

The Celebration Christian Church became independent in 1995, four years after it began.[9] We take delight in seeing our neighbors empowered, watching them develop a church that is legitimately their own.

Summary

"Paul and Barnabas appointed elders in each church and, with prayer and fasting, committed them to the Lord in whom they had put their trust" (Acts 14:23). Paul withdrew from newly-planted churches confidently, saying, "He who began a good work in you will carry it on to completion until the day of Christ Jesus" (Philippians 1:6).

Successful church planting balances pushing independence too fast with controlling the work too long. The mission has succeeded when it has:

- Developed solid leadership to deal with internal challenges; and developed stewardship, so the young church can support itself and its outreach (independence).[10]
- Instilled a vision for evangelism and equipped the church so that it will reproduce itself (reproduction).

To plant inner-city churches, which in turn plant other churches, our church-planting teams promote independence and reproducibility. The only way we can obey the Great Commission to make disciples of all people groups is to grow strong, healthy, *independent* churches (which assures quality) as quickly as possible; churches that are committed to consistent, responsible *reproduction* of additional churches in neighboring communities (which assures quantity). This is God's method for reaching the unchurched.

Independence X Reproduction = Obedience
(quality)   (quantity)   (to the Great Commission)

---

[9] World Impact is gradually phasing out our subsidy of the church's rent of our facilities.
[10] Tippet, 390.

Chapter XVI

And So Can Others:
Be Fruitful And Multiply

Each newly-planted congregation must be taught from their inception that they are not the end, but the means to an end. They must yearn to build God's Kingdom and to plant other urban churches, which will function and reproduce on their own.

The church-planting team of Celebration Christian Church spawned two additional church plants, one in South-Central Los Angeles, led by Enrique Santis, a member of the Celebration Christian Church-plant team, and the other in Wichita, Kansas, led by Fred Stoesz, the leader of the Los Angeles church-plant team.

Ministerio Pan De Vida[1]

Once the Celebration Christian Church was launched, Enrique and Silvia Santis felt released to plant another church. World Impact missionaries invited the Santises to a Thanksgiving dinner after which 12 people accepted Christ, including four adult members of a single neighborhood family.

Then, Enrique and Silvia sought and received World Impact's approval to plant a church at 50th Street. They began to assemble a church-plant team, which included Linda Burden, Pilar Gonzales and Nic and Kathryn Nelson.

---

[1]   Bread of Life Ministry.

Young Nak Presbyterian Church, a Los Angeles Korean congregation, partnered with us in this church plant. Young Nak helped finance the Santises and sent several members to share Christ with people, door-to-door, in this unchurched Spanish-speaking neighborhood. The first day, 20 families expressed a willingness to host a Bible study in their home.

Young Nak also agreed to provide the music for an evangelistic outreach in South Park (a notorious, drug-infested venue), after which Enrique would preach. The Korean choir arrived precisely at 3:00 p.m. dressed in blue robes with gold sashes. Enrique was a bit concerned about how his laid-back community would accept this formal Korean choir—until they sang their worship songs in impeccable Spanish!

As the gospel was sung and declared, people accepted Jesus as their Savior and *Ministerio Pan de Vida*, a Spanish-language cell church, was birthed.

Maria

One of their first converts was 48-year-old Maria. Maria desperately needed Jesus and a group of His disciples (a church) who would love her. She needed a spiritual home where she could feel comfortable.

Maria came to Los Angeles from El Salvador as a teenager after an arranged marriage to an older man she had never met. Her husband was domineering and abusive. He beat Maria and swore at her and their four children. He smashed their phone with a hammer when Maria tried to call the police during a family fight. He fist-fought with their oldest son, who had joined a gang. Eventually, Maria's husband was confined to a wheelchair, dying of Lou Gehrig's disease.

Maria had lived in the United States for 26 years but spoke only a few words of English. She had never driven a car, had never had a checking account and had no photo identification. Maria was alienated from God, from other races and classes, and geographically separated from her homeland and family.

When Enrique introduced himself, Maria stared out from behind her screen door. She was reluctant to smile at a stranger but was relieved to hear him speak Spanish. Enrique listened while Maria shared her struggles, her loneliness and her constant prayers to God for help and strength. Then Enrique prayed for Maria and invited her to study the Bible for herself.

Eagerly, Maria agreed to attend a home Bible study in her neighborhood. For the first time in her life she began to understand the God she had prayed to blindly for so many years. Since Maria had only a second-grade education from her native El Salvador she was reluctant to read in front of others, and was shy and soft-spoken. Her poor vision hindered her reading even further. But Maria soon accepted Christ.

Within two years of joining *Ministerio Pan de Vida*, Maria was comfortably reading her large-print Spanish Bible and had become a vocal participant in worship. She also had learned basic bookkeeping and how to work with decimals. She was ordained as the first deaconess in the church and was elected to be the first church treasurer. Now she wants to get a driver's license so she can drive a van for the church.

Maria's two oldest children, Rudy and Christina, gang veterans, have both married, largely in response to Maria's new-found, faith-centered values. Her oldest son accepted Christ because of her witness. He faithfully attended church, distanced himself from his gang and worked hard to support his wife and two young children. Maria's 19 year-old twin sons, Christian and Aliro, avoided gangs through World Impact Bible clubs, and Aliro became the first member of his family to graduate from high school.

God miraculously changed Maria and her children because of their faith in Christ and involvement in *Ministerio Pan de Vida*. Maria has been transformed from a shy, reclusive and abused woman into a respected servant-leader in the emerging church.

Multiplying Cells

Pan de Vida sponsors small, weeknight, home meetings of eight to sixteen people, and offers weekly services on Friday nights as well as periodic large group gatherings to celebrate Christmas, Easter and *Pan de Vida's* anniversary. The pastor of the largest church in the world says, "In big cities nothing surpasses the small group for effective penetration of every apartment building, language group, social class and neighborhood."[2] Home churches allow for flexibility in rapidly changing communities.

Pan de Vida seeks to multiply the cells (small group meetings held in homes) as soon as possible. Splitting the groups helps ensure continued growth by making room for new converts and by encouraging additional indigenous leaders to emerge. Many impoverished people are reluctant to lead big crowds, but feel comfortable presiding over small groups. The new church is better off with ten groups of ten, than one group of 100.

Enrique and Nic Nelson worked hard to attract whole families, particularly husbands. They invited men and their families into their homes for dinner, where relationships formed. Several men accepted Christ and were later trained as church leaders.

Forty year-old Manuel was elected the first president of *Ministerio Pan de Vida*. Manuel grew up in East Los Angeles, where he had been involved in gangs. After serving in the Navy as a fireman, he worked as a mechanic for the Los Angeles Fire Department but lost his job due to intense spiritual oppression.

When Enrique prayed against Manuel's torment, he accepted Christ and was freed from this terror. Manuel is humble and teachable, and has quickly risen to leadership.

Another church member, Ricardo, was also caught up in gangs, crime, alcohol and violence. He accepted Christ and was baptized. Then, one by one, his extended family accepted the Lord and joined home Bible studies. Ricardo is on fire for the

---

2   Paul Yonggi Cho, *Successful Home Cell Groups.* (South Plainfield, NJ: Bridge Publishing, 1981).

Lord and has grown into a Christian leader. He and his wife started a cell group in their apartment.

More Is Better

Reproduction is contagious—it may be inevitable. *Pan de Vida* expects to start satellite cells in various parts of Los Angeles, as evangelism proceeds along family lines and friendships.

Let me give you an example of how this sort of reproduction happens. In 1988, Gerardo Lara moved to Los Angeles from Mexico with his wife and two children. His children joined World Impact Bible Clubs and later entered our Los Angeles Christian School.

Gerardo came to a Celebration Christian Church retreat at THE OAKS, World Impact's camp, with members of the Spanish-speaking congregation. There Gerardo received Christ, was later baptized, and has since become a church elder.

In 1996, Gerardo's relatives, who knew of his now-solid faith in Christ, asked him to come to Mexico City to pray for his teenage niece, Elena. She had been exposed to witchcraft as a child and now, years later, was exhibiting strange behavior.

Gerardo invited Enrique Santis to accompany him to Mexico City. Gerardo's plane fare was covered by a special collection from the Celebration Christian Church; Enrique's was paid for through the sacrificial giving of his friends at *Pan de Vida*.

Enrique instructed Gerardo's relatives to invite everyone from their extended family and surrounding community who cared about Elena to their home. Over 35 people crowded into the small room as Enrique began to pray for Elena. In a dramatic scene of demonic deliverance, God freed Elena from spiritual oppression in the presence of those gathered. Then Enrique invited the witnesses to receive Christ into their hearts by faith. Everyone in the room joined Enrique in the sinner's prayer to accept Jesus. Like a page from the book of Acts, Enrique and Gerardo prayed and counseled people through the dinner hours and late into the night.

When Enrique and Gerardo awoke the next morning, there was a long line of people waiting to pray with them. Enrique instructed the people to bring their magical amulets and charms for destruction as a sign of their trust in the power of Christ to free them from evil powers. After three days of ministry, seeds were planted for what we pray will become a new church in Mexico.

The fruit of our Los Angeles ministry reached people in Mexico City far more effectively than if Anglos had gone there to minister. Gerardo, a first generation link with Mexico, returned to his country with the power of the gospel. In a few days, Christ used him to lead scores of people to Jesus, a process that might have stretched into years for a foreign missionary.

United At The Cross Community Church

In 1994, Fred Stoesz and his family relocated to Wichita, Kansas after 19 years of ministry with World Impact in South-Central Los Angeles (where they planted the Celebration Christian Church) and a year in Guatemala (for further language training). Their vision for church planting in the city continued.

Fred is from the Mennonite Brethren tradition. In 1994, leaders of his denomination asked him to partner with them in church planting in a poor community of Hispanic Americans, African Americans and Anglos. Fred was intrigued, believing with all his heart that God's standard for the Church is inclusiveness. (See *Addendum E*).

Fred knew that in the Church: "There is no Greek or Jew, circumcised or uncircumcised, barbarian or Scythian, slave or free, but only Christ is all, and is in all" (Colossians 3:11). The gospel transcends every obstacle and offers healing for every division in society—culture, race, gender, nationality or class— by forming one body. In Christ, diverse and alien people find unity.

What a promise for our cities! In Christ, we are all one. No more African, Asian, Caucasian or Hispanic. No rich or poor. No male or female. We are one! This is revolutionary.

Fred Stoesz knew that racial unity in the Church is central to fulfilling the Great Commission. Our love for one another is how the world will know God. It is how Christ will call people to be part of His Bride. It validates Christ's claim about Himself.[3]

This opportunity in Wichita could demonstrate the unifying power of the gospel. Armed with this theological truth, Fred assembled a church-plant team and jumped into the target community head first.

The neighborhood had two low-income housing units with a total of 180 families. World Impact provided the missionary staff; the Mennonite Brethren offered start-up money, resources and volunteer manpower.

In August, 1995, Fred's church-plant team conducted a week of children's and family ministries in this community, attended by 70 children and 23 families. Sixteen children and teenagers accepted Christ. Eleven families indicated an interest in starting a church. Some had been praying for a community church for years, and excitedly asked Fred after their Friday night program, "So when are we starting church services?"

That September, Fred and Jolene Stoesz, three other World Impact missionaries, and seven community families began meeting for teaching and prayer. God brought Black, White and Hispanic families to a church that boldly declares the reconciling power of the cross to a watching neighborhood.

In December, 1995, the new church had their first baptism, celebrated their first Christmas together and had their first communion service. The members chose the name, "United At The Cross Community Church."

Pablo, from El Salvador, aspires to be a pastor. Sitting under Fred's teaching, Pablo is learning how to teach and preach God's Word. Other church members teach Bible classes for children, contribute financially and attend every prayer meeting and worship service. We believe that by the summer of 1997 (two years after starting) this church will be on its way to independence.

---

[3] "May they be brought to complete unity to let the world know that You sent me and have loved them even as You have loved me" (John 17:23).

Church planting creates new and thriving communities of believers, raising the spiritual dead and seating them with Christ in the heavenly realms (Ephesians 2:1,6). It reconciles the alienated and makes them into a family, a free-standing social structure, a holy temple in which God dwells by His Spirit (Ephesians 2:19-22).

Church planting is God's work. Our plans are worthless apart from a mighty outpouring of God's Spirit. Our intimate relationship to Jesus (*who we are* individually and corporately) is the foundation upon which our mission strategy (*what we do*) is built. (See *Addendum A*).

The Power Of Multiplication

The devil would love to institutionalize the Church—to steal our dynamism and instill a contentment in Christians to minister in only one location. For example, he would probably make a deal to let the Celebration Christian Church prosper at 20th and Vermont, significantly impacting people two blocks in every direction, if we abandoned all other Los Angeles neighborhoods.

But we will not deal with the devil. We will not trade a fortress of hundreds of believers for millions remaining unreached. We are planning to take entire cities for God, neighborhood by neighborhood. We believe this will happen as God's movement of revival comes and as thousands of believers adopt this same commitment.[4]

The following chart illustrates the potential of church growth. If one World Impact church-plant team birthed one new church every two years (World Impact birthed churches are indicated on the chart as $\boxed{\frac{WI}{2}}, \boxed{\frac{WI}{4}}, \boxed{\frac{WI}{6}}, \boxed{\frac{WI}{8}}$ and $\boxed{\frac{WI}{10}}$), and each church that was planted joined us in birthing another new church every two years (indicated as ②,④,⑥,⑧ and ⑩), at the end of 10 years, we would have birthed *31* churches; at the end of 20 years, we would have birthed *1023* churches.

---

[4] Excellent books about spiritual disciplines and warfare have been written by Ed Silvoso, Peter Wagner, John Dawson and Richard Foster.

Church Growth Potential

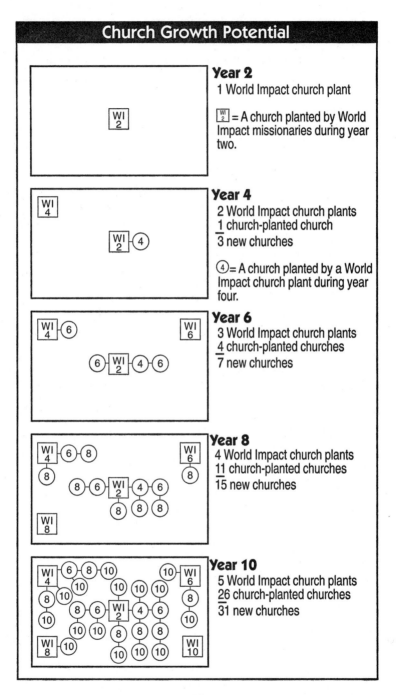

Year 2

1 World Impact church plant

W/2 = A church planted by World Impact missionaries during year two.

Year 4

2 World Impact church plants
1 church-planted church
3 new churches

④ = A church planted by a World Impact church plant during year four.

Year 6

3 World Impact church plants
4 church-planted churches
7 new churches

Year 8

4 World Impact church plants
11 church-planted churches
15 new churches

Year 10

5 World Impact church plants
26 church-planted churches
31 new churches

If we started with five church-plant teams in Los Angeles, we could birth *155* churches in 10 years and *5115* in 20 years. Today we have close to 200 missionaries nationwide who are strategically thinking, instructing and promoting the planting of independent and reproducible churches, so that we can take our cities for God.

Chapter XVII

Let The Spirit Come

The city will remain alienated until "the Spirit is poured upon us from on high" (Isaiah 32:15). Then the spiritual desert will become fertile and "God's" people will live in peace.

Let the Spirit come!

Let the desert bloom with poppies, lupines, bougainvillea, orchids, roses and hibiscus! Who cares if they grow out of cracks in rocks, on the mountains or in the plains? Where matters little when the desert bursts into bloom. It glorifies God!

Let us train leadership from the urban poor, and equip them to plant and lead churches for the urban poor, as rapidly as possible. Let us affirm every biblical model that dynamically reproduces churches.

Let the Spirit come.

Let ten thousand churches bloom. Let them birth a hundred thousand more. Let them grow in the shanties, flourish in the housing projects, multiply in the recreation centers. Let them revive abandoned cathedrals.

Let the Spirit come!

Now, let us examine three different species of urban wildflower church, each distinct in its beauty, all heady with the aroma of Christ. The bouquet of blooms shares one Lord, one faith, one baptism.

Let the Spirit come!

Military Avenue Evangelical Presbyterian Church (EPC)

When Rev. Randy Brown arrived at Military Avenue EPC in 1989 it had only ten members—down from several hundred in the 1940's. Southwest Detroit was plagued by poverty, homelessness and unemployment.

Randy employed the Beachhead strategy in order to use the structures of traditional ministry in urban church planting. It is based upon military tactics for taking enemy territory[1] and has three phases:

1. Establish a strong *supply line* of missionaries, prayer, spiritual encouragement, leadership, volunteers and financial support from existing churches. Randy's supply line initially came out of the Evangelical Presbyterian denomination. Military Avenue Church began to grow when it had resources to reach out to more people in the community through children's clubs, a food program and a teen ministry.

2. Develop a *beachhead,* a position of strength, as a base of operation in enemy territory. Randy urged the EPC to go farther than securing a single church with a single minister in the city. The EPC responded by arranging a meeting between Randy and me at the EPC headquarters in Livonia, Michigan. In 1994, World Impact and the Evangelical Presbyterian Church formed a cooperative relationship to reinvigorate Military Avenue Evangelical Presbyterian Church.

Through this relationship our work in Detroit began to establish a position of strength. Dave and Marijane Grimaldo joined Randy and Barb Brown to form our initial team. They reach nearly a thousand different community people each year. God has birthed a worshiping congregation of a hundred, the majority of whom are C_1 (urban poor). This beachhead is used to evangelize, disciple and develop leaders, who are crucial for the third stage, the development of future churches.

Let me introduce you to three godly leaders:

---

[1] Satan's territory, "For our struggle is not against flesh and blood but against...the powers of this dark world and against the spiritual forces of evil in the heavenly realms" (Ephesians 6:12).

Wally came to church for the first time in 25 years covered with oily dirt and smelling like gasoline. We were glad he joined us. (Two decades earlier Wally had worn the same type of clothes to church and was asked to leave until he could dress appropriately.) Wally kept coming to our church even though he had a drug habit, which had cost him his home and family. He lived in a rusted-out van and hung out on the streets with other drug addicts and prostitutes.

But the gospel of Jesus affected Wally. One night while he was sleeping in his van, God let Wally know that if he did not turn to Christ, he would die. Wally came back to church, and for the first time, he came to God. He hungered for the Word of God, so he read through his Bible once, and when he finished, he read it again.

Today Wally is part of our church. He is being discipled to preach the Word of God. He loves to share Jesus in places where others would not set foot. God has made a difference in Wally's life through a church in the inner city which reached the poor.

When _Jim_ was 11-years-old, his mom and dad left him and his brothers and sisters. Jim became a parent to his siblings, taking any job to help care for his family. He came to our church because we gave out food. He was fed, and he heard the message of Jesus. Jim began to feel different. He wanted to come to church, get into a Bible study and do anything to keep feeling the loving embrace of Jesus. Jim is now being discipled in a small group of leaders. Pastor Brown is often amazed at Jim's wisdom.

We met _Robert_ through his brother, who was in a gang. A couple of years ago his brother went to prison for killing a rival gang member. But Robert was different. Dave Grimaldo, a World Impact missionary, became Robert's friend. Dave made sure that Robert was in his Thursday Bible club, a place where teens might suck a bowl of Jell-O through a straw or beat each other with socks filled with flour. No matter how much fun they have, they always are challenged to come to Jesus. One night at Dave's club, Robert gave his life to Christ.

Robert is in church every Sunday, without parents; in spite of his peers, he is there. Dave has had a profound effect on Robert. Gangs are often connected to families. Brothers follow brothers into gangs. Robert found a different brother to follow, Dave Grimaldo. Instead of leading Robert to jail, Dave is leading Robert to a bright future.

Our beachhead in Detroit now consists of a mother church with several young leaders, a career-development center and a host of other programs that minister to the whole person. We are building a family center that will be instrumental in securing our position of strength.

3. Finally, *church-plant teams* are sent out from the beachhead deeper into enemy territory. As new churches are planted, the beachhead empowers young developing churches, offering ongoing support to them without the cost of duplicating resources. For example, church planters come to the beachhead for biblical training, schooling for children, food programs and career development. The result is multiple churches sharing the gospel of Jesus and being empowered to minister to the needs of their congregations through the programs at the beachhead.

Let the Spirit come and empower His Church!

Refuge In Christ Church

In 1988, we started a ministry in Chester, Pennsylvania, an impoverished, predominantly African-American city outside Philadelphia. Our Director, Michael Freeman, launched a church plant across the street from his home in McCaffery Village Housing Development.

Mike began a Bible study and worked hard to evangelize and disciple community adults. Some potential leaders disqualified themselves through sexual immorality and were unwilling to repent. Others left to work elsewhere. With few indigenous leaders, the church's growth stagnated.

However, Mike persevered and trusted God to provide indigenous leaders. Soon, God called Gerry Covert, a committed Christian from the community, to work with Mike's church because it was reaching the unsaved. Gerry was then joined by several others from within the church in forming a leadership committee to guide the church.

Upon the new church leaders' initiative, the church building received a fresh coat of paint, new flower arrangements and an improved sound system. They started a Sunday school at "their" church and showed signs of readiness to receive the "responsibility of leading" baton from the missionaries!

Mike began the church plant under the name, "McCaffery Village Community Church," hoping to give church members a sense of ownership. However, the new leadership team changed the name to, "Refuge in Christ Church." They felt the original name caused some people to think they had to live in McCaffery Village to be a member of the church. They wanted anyone seeking Christ to feel welcome.

As a first step in breaking down barriers dividing their community, the church held outdoor services on a slab of cement in the middle of the McCaffery Village Housing Project. Fifteen new people came, and four adults recommitted their lives to Christ.

Another Sunday, the church took their worship service to the Community Center of nearby Lamokin Village Housing Development. There is an unwritten rule about not crossing into the territory of another housing development, but the church members from McCaffery Village wanted to penetrate that invisible barrier in order to reach people in Lamokin Village for Christ.

The Lamokin outreach drew in Keith Bradley, who recalls, "I was walking my dog and heard music from the community center. So we stepped inside and I saw my cousin, Tyrone, at the podium praising the Lord. A neighbor, Joyce Story, told me to come on in, so I took my dog home and came back."

Recently, Molly came to church to seek comfort from God in the midst of a tragedy. She told the members, "My mind was made up on coming here, because when you say come as you are, you mean come as you are, church clothes or not." Molly's experience illustrates the value of the church being accessible and approachable to people who have often felt alienated from the Church.

Let the Spirit come! Let Him heal the brokenhearted!

Three Cultures In One Neighborhood

When we started a ministry in Pueblo del Rio Housing Project in South-Central Los Angeles in the late 1960's, the community was entirely African American (monocultural). However, today it is one-third Black, one-third Spanish-speaking Latinos (including separate Mexican, Guatemalan, El Salvadoran and Nicaraguan groups) and one-third Laotian Hmong.

Willie, an African American, is a third-generation resident of Pueblo. His roots go back to the South, but most of his family memories surround the railroad tracks of this federal housing project. He lives with his grandmother, six brothers, four cousins and two nephews.

Jorge was born in El Salvador. His parents fled to the United States seeking refuge from an oppressive regime. He is excited to live here but afraid of neighborhood bullies. He has been shot at and seen many of his friends killed in gang wars. He is afraid to walk in some parts of the projects because of his past involvement with gangs.

Singsong is from Cambodia. He lives with his parents, sister, brother and an uncle. He understands little English and is overwhelmed by the dense population, the steady traffic and constant noise.

We want all three of these boys and their extended families to confess Jesus as Savior. Since we are committed to planting a church in this multicultural neighborhood, must that congregation be as ethnically diverse as the neighborhood? The goal is admirable as long as people are not forced to change cultures in order to become Christians, or to join a church (Acts 15).

God meets people in their own culture. Christianity is not like Islam, where a convert must learn Arabic. There is no requirement for a Christian to master Hebrew, Greek or Latin.

The gospel is preached and God is worshiped in every culture and tongue.

Most mature believers have been discipled within their own culture. Later, missionaries share those biblical principles cross-culturally. The gospel spreads most naturally through homogeneous people groups when listeners hear God's call in their heart language and in their natural surroundings.[2]

How does the Church balance the common identity Christians have with Christ (inclusiveness), with respecting a people group's cultural heritage (cultural neutrality)? The prevailing principle is that a person should never be forced by us to change cultures in order to become a Christian. For example, a Laotian should not have to learn Spanish in order to worship God.

At the same time, an English-speaking African-American congregation must welcome, and bend over backwards to accommodate, a Guatemalan or a Cambodian visitor, new believer or potential member. Ideally, a church should eventually reflect the neighborhood's ethnic diversity as a prophetic witness of peace and harmony among the races and cultures. In the Church, people groups can mix and still maintain their cultural identity (as Guatemalans or Hmong), especially in the first generation.[3]

While established multi-ethnic churches adapt more readily to changing neighborhoods and can more easily welcome new people from different races or cultures, new believers usually feel most comfortable in a congregation that is culturally homogeneous.

While there is no one correct method, let me share our strategy for church planting at Pueblo del Rio—a community that encompasses three different languages and more than three distinct cultures.

---

2   Harvie Conn, *A Clarified Vision For Urban Ministry* (Grand Rapids, MI: Zondervan, 1987) 216.

3   Frequently, second-generation ethnics become part of the dominant culture, or form their own new culture, as racial or ethnic distinctions wane in importance. Intermarriages and extensive exposure to other peoples leads to more comfort with ethnic diversity.

After scores of children accepted Christ, Bismark Nwadike, our church planter in the community, began to share the gospel with their parents. As a result of that, 55 adults have been incorporated into *cell groups,* or house churches. Each cell evidences witness, fellowship, worship and stewardship (Acts 2:41-47). Nurture is the strength of cell groups. These cells are homogeneous. One cell is made up primarily of African Americans and another of Guatemalans.

As these cells mature in Christ, they will become committed to a larger *congregation,* which will be composed of cell groups with language or ethnic homogeneity—here Guatemalans, Nicaraguans, Mexicans and Cubans can enjoy worship, teaching and evangelism together linked by their common use of Spanish.

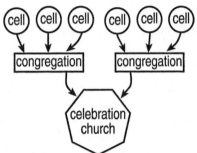

Finally, we pray that God will create a *celebration,* or the *Church* at Pueblo del Rio, composed of multiple congregations in the community. They come together for baptism, communion, Christmas, New Years, Thanksgiving or other special events. Each celebration should reflect the ethnic and language composition of the entire neighborhood. Our oneness in Christ should be celebrated. We are different folds, but part of one flock with one Shepherd (John 10:16).

Pueblo demonstrates the beauty and complexity of planting churches in ethnically-diverse urban communities. Two biblical principles—inclusiveness and cultural neutrality—seem to stand in tension.

Inclusiveness says, "Whosoever will may come to Christ's Church"—African American, Hispanic American, Native American, Asian American, Anglo, rich, poor, male, female—all are welcome.

Cultural Neutrality says, "Just as you are." Willie can remain an African American; Jorge, a Latino; and Singsong, a Cambodian.

Both principles are true. But the potential complications from obeying these truths could tax the wisdom of Solomon. For example, if everyone is welcome and no one has to change in order to be part of the Church, which language is spoken? Which culture is dominant? Which holidays are celebrated?

Trying to balance these two principles has caused missiologists Excedrin headaches for generations. Frequently, one principle is literally observed, while the other is merely paid lip service. If the Church is going to prosper in the city it must understand and learn to live with this antinomy.[4]

That means that, while no one in Pueblo needs to change cultures to become a Christian, the ultimate goal of every individual believer is to be a prophetic witness to the neighborhood of how multiple races and cultures can be one in Christ. God's challenge to us is to be the first to accept those who are different, to make allowances for those who do not fit into our church, to give way when cultures clash in our church. That witness promises to be a dynamic method of evangelism for the urban Church in the 21st century. Non believers will be attracted to a Church where all are genuinely welcomed and respected.

In the early Church, every community had several cells and multiple congregations, but in each city there was only one Church. Paul did not write to the cell at Athens and Second Street, nor to the Cushite, Scythian or Italian congregation, but to the Church in Ephesus. The cells related to and supported each other, and viewed themselves inclusively as the Church.

The universality of the Church does not mean assimilation in the sense of losing cultural distinctions. Revelation describes every tribe, language, people and nation worshiping God. Even the Godhead celebrates an eternal diversity within unity.

---

[4] An antinomy occurs when two truths appear to the human mind to contradict each other, but blend beautifully from God's perspective. The tension between salvation by faith, or by works, is an example. In such a case, it is the duty of the Christian to affirm both principles and to seek God's guidance in obeying both truths.

Let the Spirit come! Let Him promote evangelism and discipleship among the urban poor. Let indigenous leadership be raised up and new churches be planted.

Let the Spirit come!

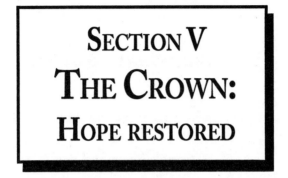

SECTION V
THE CROWN:
HOPE RESTORED

Proverbs 13:12 says, "Hope deferred makes the heart sick, but a longing fulfilled is a tree of life." Jesus restores our hope He heals our sickness and satisfies our longing.

The Church is an equal-opportunity liberator. As the urban poor find hope in Christ, they will be numbered in that great multitude crying before the throne, "Salvation belongs to our God, who sits on the throne, and to the Lamb" (Revelation 7:10). Planting churches in urban America transforms, heals and renews the urban poor!

Chapter XVIII

You Should Be Involved

There may be a tragic situation in St. Louis of which I am completely unaware, My ignorance lessens my responsibility. Racial genocide in Bosnia is so far away that I have neither the influence nor the ability to respond. My lack of proximity limits my culpability.

But when I hear the groans of the urban poor or the cries of racism and oppression *in my city,* I am responsible, especially when I know the problem (alienation) and the solution (reconciliation to God and our fellow man). Once I know the problem and the solution, I will either be part of the problem or part of the solution. Inaction endorses the status quo.

You may be saying, "That's okay for you, Keith, but when I think about the urban poor I see huge barriers—a racial difference and/or a class distinction (the haves versus the have nots), among others. I am scared of the city. I don't even like the city. I am not sure God could use me there."

What Difference Does It Make Whether Or Not I Am Involved With The Poor And Oppressed?

The difference is practical and eternal.

From a *practical* standpoint, there is more scripture encouraging God's people to lovingly relate to the poor and oppressed than any other subject in the Bible. God is concerned that our actions accurately reflect His heart of compassion for the hurting in our society. Hundreds of biblical promises are contingent upon "feeding the hungry, or caring for the orphan, the widow, the stranger, the alien, the prisoner." Many of the wonderful blessings that God wishes to shower upon His people are forfeited because we fail to meet the contingency of ministering to the poor or oppressed. Proverbs 21:13 says, "Those who turn a deaf ear to the poor will have their cries ignored in their time of need."

Eternally, God is not willing that any should perish. Our world is becoming more and more populated by the urban poor and oppressed. Every Christian should be declaring the good news to the poor, healing the broken-hearted and setting the captive free. We need to walk in the footsteps of the One whose name the Church bears.

Further, if Christians are racially or socially divided, the world will be repelled by our hypocrisy. Racial and class unity in the Church draws people to God. Our unity may be the single greatest tool for evangelism in our fragmented generation.

Who Can Be Involved?

Every Christian can help expand God's Bride in the city. All cultures, genders, races, nationalities and classes must participate in church planting. Erastus, the City Treasurer of Corinth (C_3); Paul, the bicultural missionary (C_2); and Quartus, a slave or former slave (C_1) all planted churches. God used Claudia, Tryphena and Tryphosa, women from Rome. And this was in a sexist, class-conscious, racist, nationalistic society.

Some church-planting team members sat with Paul in jail; others traveled with him. Many prayed for him; several gave money; others took dictation from Paul or communicated on his behalf, i.e., walked to another city with a message. Many evangelized and taught. People with all kinds of gifts helped to reach the unchurched.

God can use you.

How Can You Be Involved?

You can pray

Pray for church-planting team members and the target community. You can take prayer walks through the community, asking God to open the hearts of men and women, who live there, to the gospel. If we humble ourselves and pray, and seek God's face and turn from our wicked ways, God will hear our prayers and heal our land (II Chronicles 7:14).[1]

You can give

You can financially support a church-planting team, allowing missionaries to focus their energies on evangelism and discipleship. Where your treasure is, there your heart will be also.

I spoke at the 1996 Promise Keepers Conference in Boise, Idaho. As I talked, I introduced a White pastor whose church had been given a facility where they could worship ten years before. God blessed their ministry and expanded their congregation so that they needed to build a new sanctuary. They planned to use the money from the sale of their old sanctuary as a down payment.

Meanwhile, a Black congregation looked at the church, but could not afford it. They prayed over the church, marched around it, hoping the price would fall, like Jericho's walls, and asked God for a miracle—but they hardly expected one.

Then the Spirit of God moved. An elder in the White congregation said, "Freely we have received, freely give. I move that we donate the sanctuary to the Black congregation." Another elder seconded the motion, and it was carried unanimously. When the White pastor symbolically[2] gave the keys to the

---

[1] Steve Hawthorne and Graham Kendrick, *Prayer-Walking: Praying on Site With Insight* (Orlando, FL: Creative, Inc., 1993) and John Dawson, *Taking Our Cities for God: How to Break Down Spiritual Strongholds* (Orlando, FL: Creative, Inc., 1990).

[2] They had given the church to the African-American congregation earlier.

church to the Black pastor on stage at Promise Keepers, thousands of men responded with a standing ovation.

If you have freely received, you have an opportunity to freely give. If God has blessed you, you can become an integral part of a missionary team by financially supporting it. Your commitment will empower the urban poor.

You can come plant churches

If you want to be involved in a mighty movement of God's Spirit, you can plant churches among the urban poor. You can *volunteer* for a few hours or one day a week, or for a few months. You might take ethnographic or demographic surveys, help canvas a community with door-to-door evangelism or teach Bible studies or Bible clubs.[3]

You can come as a *full-time church planter.*[4] Capture the exciting dynamics of first-century Christianity by sharing the amazing gospel with unreached peoples, watching the mighty power of God's Spirit release your new friends from bondage, training them to grow strong in Christ and teaching them to boldly share the gospel with others.[5]

You can walk in the shoes of Paul; enjoy the fellowship of Philip, Silas and Timothy; be on the cutting edge of the gospel; make a difference for eternity; leave a legacy.

God can use you. All kinds of saints walk with Jesus: illiterate and scholarly, rich and poor, male and female, Jew and Gentile, Black and White. No matter. In Christ we are one.

You could join us in planting a congregation like the Watts Agapeland Church. Seventy-five people and 20 families attend.

---

[3] In addition to prayer, service examples include food distribution, maintenance, custodial work, construction, building repairs, painting, legal or clerical services, landscaping, medical or dental service, auto repair, tutoring or literacy programs; job-training mentoring, graphic arts, financial counseling/planning, real estate management, thrift store clothes sorting, computer data entry, athletic recreation, English-as-a-second language help or small-business entrepreneurship.

[4] Career missionaries move into the community to help plant the church.

[5] Denominations, individual churches, Sunday school classes and college groups can partner with a church-plant team, or form their own church-plant team. World Impact will assist interested churches.

Every one of the 15 men and their pastor has served time in the state or federal penitentiary.

God is setting the captives free. These former prisoners have a vision to plant churches in every housing project in Watts.

Early Christians found peace in Jesus and overflowed with joy—some in jail, many in slavery or poverty, several in the Coliseum. Their condition did not matter, because their position (in Christ) was secure.

You can be part of ending the alienation and hopelessness among the urban poor. Does the task seem overwhelming? Too many obstacles? Impossible? Hear the words of young David going to battle against the giant of his day: "You come against me with sword and spear and javelin, but I come against you in the name of the Lord Almighty" (I Samuel 17:45).

Come plant churches among the poor. Come join the company of the committed. In the mighty name of Jesus, "bestow on them a crown of beauty instead of ashes" (Isaiah 61:3).

A CROWN OF BEAUTY

Out of Ashes...A Crown of Beauty.

Ashes is a sign of death. A crown is the headdress of joy.

A crown connotes status and authority—winners of athletic events, kings, priests, God's people wear crowns.

New Christians were Paul's crown (I Thessalonians 2:19). A bride of noble character is her husband's crown (Proverbs 12:4). One day Christ will be crowned with many crowns (Revelation 19:12)!

Could it be that the *many crowns* that adorn the King of Kings are made from ashes that He transformed into crowns of beauty? Is it not possible that the poor, for whom Jesus came to preach the Good News, should adorn Him for eternity?

Ashes to crowns, like coal to diamonds. Only God could do such things.

Addendum A

World Impact's Purpose:
Our Biblical Basis For Ministry

A blessing (sometimes a hazard) of preaching in numerous locations is that I frequently depend on someone else to drive me to the church, convention or university where I am speaking.

One Sunday morning, I was picked up by an enthusiastic volunteer from a college which I was to address on Monday. She was to transport me to a rural church where I was scheduled to preach that Sunday.

After exchanging normal niceties, I asked the lady if she knew where the church was, and how long it would take to get there. She assured me that she had excellent directions and that the church was about 45 minutes out in the country.

We did fine until we got to the geographically-described landmarks, i.e., the first cluster of trees on your right, followed by the large red water tower. We saw a tower, but it was not red. About 10:55 a.m., I started to worry that we would be late.

By 11:10 a.m., we thought we had found the *red* water tower and proceeded quickly down the adjacent country road. We did turn left at the second gravel road, passed three barns and made a right turn just past the school house, but there was nothing in front of us. The directions said we would run into a numbered county road, but we drove on and on.

Suddenly, we spotted a church. My driver triumphantly turned into the parking lot. I jumped out and hurried down the left side of the sanctuary to the front. The congregation was singing a hymn (according to the bulletin, just before I was to preach). I found the pastor on the front row, introduced myself and asked him what time the message normally ends. He said, "About 12 noon or 12:05 p.m." When the congregation completed the song, I walked to the pulpit and started to preach.

A few minutes into my message the young lady who had driven me to the church started to wave her arms from the rear of the sanctuary. Finally, she stopped. I could not understand her excitement until the message was over, and she announced that we were at the wrong church!

Knowing where you are going and how to get there is extremely important.

World Impact is a Christian missions organization, a group of believers who are committed to God, to each other and to the same purpose.

World Impact's purpose is "to glorify and honor God and to delight in Him *in the inner city.*"

Revelation 4:11 says, "You are worthy, our Lord and our God, to receive glory and honor and power; for You created all things, and by Your will they were created and have their being."

The key words are "glory" and "honor."

To "glorify" God is to *worship* Him. We worship God, adore and exalt Him, because of who He is and what He has done. God alone is holy (Revelation 15:4). David says, "Ascribe to the Lord the glory due His name" (Psalm 29:2). Paul teaches us, "So whether you eat or drink or *whatever* you do, do it all for the glory of God" (I Corinthians 10:31). Every action and thought needs to be consumed with glorifying God (Romans 12:1, 2; Psalm 71:8).

To "honor" God is to *respect* Him because of His intrinsic worth and unmatchable deeds. Solomon instructs us to "honor the Lord" (Proverbs 3:9). "To Him who sits on the throne (God), and to the Lamb (Christ) be praise and honor and glory and power for ever and ever" (Revelation 5:13).

When we glorify and honor God—when we worship and respect Him—we naturally delight in Him. To delight in God is to experience total enjoyment, extreme satisfaction, pure pleasure. Nothing can be added; He is completely sufficient. A godly person's "delight is in the law of the Lord" (Psalm 1:2; Psalm 27). Our happiness comes as we glorify and honor God.

After God saved us, He left us on earth to declare His honor and glory to others, so that they might delight in Him if they meet Him. We are not primarily on earth to make friendships, accumulate wealth, achieve popularity or gain power. When we became God's children, and died to our sinful nature, we became His servants (Galatians 2:20). We are His hands and feet and should reflect His heart for people.

God is more important than we are. Our fulfillment comes as we keep God first. "Delight yourself in the Lord" (by glorifying and honoring God—by worshiping and respecting Him), "and He will give you the desires of your heart" (Psalm 37:4).

The chief end of all people is to bring glory and honor to God, and to delight in Him. The only thing unique to World Impact is the last prepositional phrase, *"in the inner city,"* because this is where He has placed us.

Glorify +	honor =	delight in God	in the inner city
(worship)	(respect)	(total enjoyment)	(where God has placed us).

Two steps help World Impact missionaries achieve our purpose of "glorifying and honoring God and delighting in Him in the inner city."

I. The first step is **TO KNOW GOD.**

God's first commandment is to, "Love the Lord your God with all your heart and with all your soul and with all your mind and with all your strength" (Mark 12:30). Loving God means having an intimate relationship with Him (Philippians 3:10). God is more concerned about who we *are*—our character and the integrity of our heart—than with what we *do*—our actions and ministry to others.

Even though it was never said, when I was growing up, those in spiritual authority over me strongly implied that my "righteousness" was primarily determined by attendance and activity. I was "good" if I was active in my youth group, went on door-to-door evangelism and faithfully attended church. So I did as many of these things as I could in order to please God, to secure my righteousness by works.

When I went to Watts hundreds of children attended Bible clubs, and scores of youngsters accepted Christ. I received many pats on the back and words of affirmation, reinforcing righteousness by works.

So, it was disarming to realize that God is more concerned with who I *am* than with what I *do*. Even though faith without works is dead (James 2:26), all *my* works are like dung (Philippians 3:8), my "righteous acts are like filthy rags" (Isaiah 64:6). Missionaries must *be* God's people before we can *do* His work.

We are more concerned about our missionaries' character than their degrees, experience or training. Galatians 6:7 (TLB) says, "We reproduce in kind for good or evil." Just as a kangaroo cannot give birth to a squirrel, nor an apple tree produce grapes, an individual who is *not* a disciple (a godly follower of Jesus) cannot train another person to walk in the footsteps of the Messiah!

There are five primary avenues by which we get to know God and develop an intimate relationship with Him.

1. <u>Bible study</u>. "Study to shew thyself approved unto God, a workman that needeth not to be ashamed, rightly dividing the word of truth" (II Timothy 2:15, KJV). We must know and understand God's Word if we are going to know and understand God. Matthew 22:29 cautions, "You are in error because you do not know the scriptures or the power of God." We do not acquire a working knowledge of the Bible through osmosis, i.e., sitting in church or listening to other Christians.

Sometimes, when I board an airplane the flight attendant sees "Dr." in front of my name. On one flight I was reading a magazine when a stewardess asked if I could help her. I followed her up the aisle as she told me that someone had passed out. Then I explained that I was not a medical doctor, but I could pray for this individual.

Let's pretend that I am a physician, and that I have hung out my shingle in your neighborhood. One day you walk into my office thinking that you had an attack of appendicitis. Immediately I get my medical books, flip to the index and find the place where it says, "Appendix." Then I turn to the appropriate page in the book and locate a diagram illustrating the specific location of the appendix. Finally, I hold the book up to your body, comparing the sketch in the book to your abdomen, trying to verify where your appendix corresponds with the appendix sketched in the book.

How would you feel?

If I were the patient, I would be out the door looking for another doctor, who has a better idea of where my appendix is (before he attempts to remove it). A person who has to find my appendix by comparing illustrations with my abdomen is not going to touch me with a scalpel.

By the same token, missionaries need a working knowledge of God's Word. We should not be "concordance Christians." To see what I mean, try this three-question test:

Question #1. Without looking at the Table of Contents, list the 66 books of the Bible.

Question #2. Write a word, or a phrase, that describes each book of the Bible. For example, Genesis is the book of beginnings; Exodus is the book of redemption; Matthew, Jesus the King.

Question #3. Write a four-to six-point outline of each book. For example, with Genesis you might write, "Adam, Noah, Abraham, Isaac, Jacob and Joseph."

If you did as poorly on this test as I did initially, you have a superficial knowledge of the Book on which we claim to stake our lives.

God wrote His Word so that we can know Him and His will. We learn what God wants by noting direct commands, by drawing principles from the life-examples of others, and by applying those lessons to ourselves. "These things happened to them as examples and were written down as warnings for us" (I Corinthians 10:11). Bible study is essential to knowing God.

2. Scripture memorization. Two primary reasons we memorize scripture are to resist personal temptation and to prepare to counsel others.

Resisting temptation. "I have hidden your word in my heart that I might not sin against you" (Psalm 119:11). Our society is saturated with sexual and materialistic temptations. Believers cannot overcome these without God's help. Scripture memorization is the Christian's primary defense against sin. When being tempted by Satan in the wilderness, the Lord quoted scripture each time to overcome temptation. God's Word warns us against evil; keeping His Word provides us with a great reward (Psalm 19:11).

Counseling others. We also memorize scripture because when people ask for our advice, we can respond with God's Word, not ours. The Holy Spirit brings things to our memory that have been stored in our minds. Then we can speak the truth with authority (II Timothy 3:16-17) and allow God to move the person's heart (Hebrews 4:12-13).

3. Prayer. A relationship in which only one member speaks, stagnates. Communication involves both speaking and listening. We listen to God through Bible study, scripture memorization and meditation. We express our grief, joy, worship and praise to our Maker through prayer.

Praise. Praise unlocks our hearts and opens us to commune with God. As we praise Him, He pours His power into our hearts and renews us. It reminds us of what sort of God we serve, and clears our minds that we might order our priorities correctly.

Not long ago God reminded me of His marvelous intervention (a bumpy airline flight) which led to my meeting and eventually marrying Katie (the flight attendant). Our children are the most obvious proof of God's goodness and how great a woman Katie is.

People who meet Joshua, Paul and David are struck by their warmth, love and sensitivity. That is a direct reflection of Katie, who, while I criss-crossed the country for the Lord, walked that fine line of being mother and father; and then when I returned, becoming mom and wife.

I praise God for His goodness in giving me Katie and my boys. I praise God for my salvation, for His love, for my health, for His ministry and for just being who He is.

Petition/Intercession. I am often guilty of trying to solve problems myself, and only when I am unsuccessful, asking God to intervene. How illogical! Jesus said, "If you remain (continue daily in the faith) in me and my words remain in you, ask what ever you wish, and it will be given you" (John 15:7).

When the inner city confronts me with injustice, oppression, poverty, deceit and sinfulness, my immediate response is to try to right wrongs by personally intervening, instituting programs, calling officials or bringing pressure to bear on the offenders.

But prayer unlocks God's treasure chest for us: "Ask and it will be given to you; seek and you will find; knock and the door will be opened to you" (Matthew 7:7). Prayer is our direct chan nel to God's unlimited resources. After we pray, God may lead us to do the exact things mentioned above—or something en tirely different!

Prayer deepens our relationship with Christ. Every believer needs to spend time daily in prayer, speaking to and listening to God. We make a tragic mistake if we believe we can survive without consistent communication with our Maker. Jesus says, "I no longer call you servants, because a servant does not know his master's business. Instead I have called you friends" (John

15:15). Communicating regularly with Jesus means we will not be merely His acquaintances, but also His friends.

4. <u>Meditation</u>. Meditation is a God-consciousness, letting our thoughts dwell on the Almighty's goodness, mercy and grace, seeing things through God-colored glasses. The righteous person meditates on the Word of God day and night (Psalm 1:2). After I pray to God, I pause and meditate. He brings verses that I have memorized and passages that I have studied to my mind. In this way, He reveals His will to me. Believers meditate on God's Word and respect what it says (Psalm 119:15).

Meditation helps us view things from God's perspective. Every day as I exit the Santa Monica freeway en route to work, I see homeless people who live by the off ramp begging for money, food or work. I find it easy to rationalize that they are beyond help or maybe do not deserve my attention until I remember God's command to "Love your neighbor as yourself." Then I know I must want to walk as Jesus walked and do what He would do.

5. <u>Worship</u>. Jesus said, "Worship the Lord your God, and serve only Him" (Matthew 4:10). When I was a sophomore at UCLA, our football team was down by 12 points to USC with four minutes left in the game. Gary Beban, UCLA's quarterback, threw a long pass into the north side of the end zone which was caught for a touchdown. Within two minutes the exact same play resulted in another touchdown, and the Bruins won the game and went on to the Rose Bowl. The crowd went nuts screaming! We were yelling at the top of our voices!

This excitement is only a drop in the bucket compared to the worship God deserves. When we realize the impact of God providing a Savior for us, our only reasonable response is worship—we need to praise, love, exalt and adore our God, Who deserves it!

Everything Christians do which is acceptable to God, is worship (I Corinthians 10:31). Worship is the only fitting response of the believer to God's greatness and goodness. In addition to the whole of our lives being worship, we need regular times for concentrated private worship and joyful corporate worship. David encourages us, "Glorify the Lord with me; let us exalt His name together" (Psalm 34:3).

Regular Bible study, scripture memorization, meditation, prayer and worship are essential in order for the believer to know God and to have an intimate relationship with Him. There are no shortcuts, no easy methods. They all demand discipline and work.

Intimacy with God is a prerequisite to bearing spiritual fruit. The biblical example of the Church as the Bride of Christ, illustrates this. If a woman is physically and emotionally able and willing to bear offspring but does not have an intimate relationship with her husband, she will never have children. If Christians are not intimate with Jesus, the Bridegroom, they will never bring forth fruit.

Once you have a healthy relationship with God through Christ—once you *are* His person—then you will *do* His work. Christ's commission explains the relationship between *being* and *doing*. You "make disciples" by baptizing them in the name of the Father, the Son and the Holy Spirit. Baptism represents self death. When you are immersed under the baptismal waters, think of it as drowning. You lose control. You die.

Imagine that I was on that ill-fated 1996 TWA flight #800 that crashed off of Long Island. When the fuselage hit the ocean my lungs filled with water and I drowned. After two days, my corpse was still buried in the Atlantic Ocean when Jesus came to me and said, "Keith, I'll make a deal with you. I'll breathe into you the breath of new life—you can be born again! But, it will cost you everything you have—you will have to go any-where I ask, do anything I ask, for as long as I ask—no questions asked!"

Immediately I say, "No way. That's slavery." Then, I realize I am not in a good bargaining position, and I accept the grace of God for what it is—a gift!

Once I have died to myself (yielded control of my life to Christ), then I can be resurrected with Him to new life. The evidence of my new life (after self death) is the fruit of the Spirit and servanthood. I will go to Watts and raise a family, teach junior-high-age boys in Bible club or Sunday School—do whatever God calls me to do.

John 12:24 says, "Unless a kernel of wheat falls to the ground and dies (self death), it remains only a single seed. But if it dies, it produces many seeds (reproduction)."

II. The second step we take in order to achieve our purpose of "honoring and glorifying God and delighting in Him in the inner city" is **TO MAKE GOD KNOWN** to others. Reproduction is the second part of the Great Commission—to teach new believers "all things I have commanded you."

After heeding the first commandment (to love God), we naturally want to obey the second commandment (to love our neighbors as ourselves), which means sharing Jesus' love with our neighbors. Making God known focuses on what we do. World Impact's approach to making God known is described in Sections Three and Four of *Out of Ashes* and Addendums B and C.

Summary

World Impact's purpose is to glorify and honor God, and delight in Him in the inner city.

I. To Know God (Philippians 3:10). Who we *are*. Self death.
   A. Bible Study (II Timothy 2:15).
   B. Scripture Memorization (Psalm 119:11).
   C. Prayer (John 15:7).
   D. Meditation (Psalm 1:2).
   E. Worship (Matthew 4:10).

II. To Make Him Known (Matthew 28:18-20). What we *do*. Reproduction.
   A. Evangelism (Colossians 4:3-6; II Timothy 4:2)
   B. Follow Up (I Timothy 4:12; II Timothy 2:2, Romans 1:11)
   C. Discipleship (John 8:31)
   D. Church Planting (I Corinthians 3:10; Acts 13, 16)

Addendum B

World Impact's Compassion Ministries

1. Demonstrating the gospel through *SCHOOLS*.

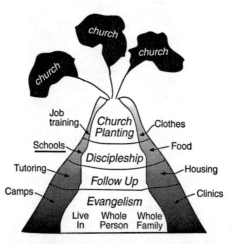

Because many of our Bible-club children have difficulty reading, we started tutoring programs.

We launched reading-readiness ministries for pre-schoolers. And because public schools in some communities where we minister consistently rank among the lowest in their states, we opened Christian schools to provide a quality education for our neighbors.

For example, in Newark, public school children go without books while School Board members attend conferences in Hawaii, buy cars for their personal use, have charge accounts at restaurants and find jobs for relatives with funds intended for students. Kids cannot read, but must attend schools that stink of urine. Children do not learn, drop out and grow up angry and resentful, deprived of a safe childhood and clean and effective schools.[1] Because of this, World Impact has a Christian elementary school in Newark, New Jersey.

In Chester, Pennsylvania, we opened the Frederick Douglass Christian School because Chester ranked last of the 501 school districts in the state. The three lowest-ranked schools in California are within a mile of our Watts Christian School. Manual Arts High School, near the Los Angeles Christian School, has the lowest graduation rate (27%) in the school district.[2]

During the 1992-1993 school year in Los Angeles 383 elementary, junior high and high school students were assaulted with deadly weapons. School officials confiscated 405 guns, 527 knives and 458 other weapons. In 1993, three high school students were shot, two fatally, on school campuses.[3]

Teachers in Los Angeles inner-city schools often suffered symptoms of combat fatigue resulting from stress caused by campus violence. One teacher had her hair set on fire by three of her students.[4]

No wonder inner-city residents have more concern for their children's safety than for their academic achievements. World Impact schools emphasize Christian character, academic competence and self confidence. They are equipping young people for a life of discipleship—a tangible demonstration of the gospel.

---

[1]   *Newark Star Ledger,* 1990's.
[2]   *San Diego Union Tribune,* Dec. 12, 1993; A33.
[3]   "Race Power and Promise in Los Angeles," 55-56.
[4]   Mary Beth Murrill, "Violence Hits Teachers, Too" *Herald Examiner,* Dec. 16, 1977.

2. Demonstrating the gospel through *JOB TRAINING*.

Most government-sponsored job-training programs have had little success in helping the hard-core unemployed gain jobs.[5] They often teach inner-city young people exactly what *not* to do to gain employment.

For example, we had teenagers "working" in the Comprehensive Employment and Training Act program, who were told by their employers to come only on Fridays after school (they were being paid to work Monday through Friday) so the students could sign their hourly wage card. This was less hassle for the employer (who was being paid to train these kids how to work) and easier for the teens (for the short term, until they realized they had learned nothing except how to cheat the system).

Because of child labor laws and the minimum wage, it was hard for our teenagers to find part-time employment without a father, aunt or employer-friend who would hire them. Still, we believed that our teenagers should learn how to work, so we tried to get them jobs.

Since 18-year-old James had accepted Christ in Watts and had nothing to do, I asked businesses if they would hire him.

5   Nathan Glazer, "A Human Capital Policy For the Cities," *The Public Interest,* No. 112, Summer, 1993: 27-49.

The manager at the Sizzler Restaurant agreed to let James be a busboy. Less than two hours after James' employment started, he showed up back in the projects, his head hanging low. He looked at me and said he got fired. I asked him why.

James reported that the manager bossed him around, told him to pick up those dishes, clean that table and wash the dirty floor. Finally, James had had enough. After all, any guy on the street who put up with such orders without resistance would be walked all over. James turned and slugged the boss square in the mouth, which ended his first venture in employment, and my relationship with the Sizzler.

It did not take long to realize that many young people with whom we worked were unemployable. So we started job-training businesses to teach teenagers how to work by working and to help them secure employment.

After listening to many employers, especially Milton Scott, a supporter who ran a textile mill outside of Atlanta, we determined that employable people show up to work (1) every day; (2) on time; (3) with a reasonably good attitude; and (4) do what they are told.

Mr. Scott pointed out that entry-level workers put much more credence in what you *do* than in what you *say*. He told new employees that they had to be at work at 8:00 a.m. sharp every morning. If they were two minutes late, in a calm, serene voice, Mr. Scott said, "You are fired." He never asked why the employee was late, because he had heard every excuse in the book, e.g., my mother is sick, they blew up the bus, the police quarantined my neighborhood.

Similarly, if a new employee missed one day of work in the first month, she, too, was fired, no questions asked. Mr. Scott learned, over the years, that if a person missed one day in the first month, she would miss more and more in succeeding months, unless something radically changed her work habits. So there was never an opportunity for excuses. He simply said, "You are fired."

When Mr. Scott terminated a person for being one minute late or missing one day of work in the first 30 days, everyone in the mill immediately understood that Mr. Scott meant what he said. Few others were late or missed a day of work.

Mr. Scott would put one red mark in the upper right-hand corner of the employment card of the newly-fired employee. If the employee returned, said he was sorry and promised to be on time (or not absent), he would be reinstated. The same cycle could be repeated one more time, but after the second red check mark, Mr. Scott would not hire the person again.

Mr. Scott was a caring Christian who loved his employees (most came from the inner city of Atlanta) and wanted them to succeed. So you can understand his pride when he took me into a room in his mill that was lined with hundreds of pictures of his former entry-level employees. Among their ranks are college presidents, bank presidents, ministers, missionaries, politicians and people who have succeeded in all walks of life. Each had started out in Scottsdale—in a textile mill. All had been trained by a Christian employer.

Mr. Scott also explained that to help an unemployable person become employable you need entry-level jobs that are:

1. Highly repetitive. Doing the same thing over and over again instills discipline.

2. Easily measurable. It is not good to have a job where two people can have different opinions regarding its completion. For example, if I tell a young person to clean a room, and he says he is done, we might have a discussion about the definition of "clean." But if I ask him to screw the tops onto 100 salt shakers, they are either screwed on, or they are not. We need "widgets" that are easily measurable.

3. Relatively safe. A young person should be safe while learning how to work.

4. Able to be done on site. It is the teenager's responsibility to arrive at work on time, not our responsibility to awaken him, pick him up and transport him somewhere.

Our job trainees have separated nuts, bolts and screws; made knee pads; and assembled sprinkler heads for an irrigation company. Many of our graduates have become productive employees.

Several of our ministries (a medical/dental clinic, camps, food and clothing distribution) have tasks that need to be done in order to operate, i.e., sales, sorting, inventory, janitorial, gardening and cooking. We use these opportunities to train our neighbors how to work and help them acquire marketable skills. Delivering a service of compassion while training someone how to work is a win-win situation.

A splendid example are our thrift stores, or outlet stores, which sell used or new clothes at reduced prices to our neighbors. We train community people to run the stores. We charge enough for the clothes to cover the cost of our employees' salaries and overhead.

Our Good Samaritan Clinic in Wichita, Kansas delivers medical and dental services to the surrounding urban community. Neighborhood residents are employed as receptionists and medical assistants.

3. Demonstrate the gospel through *CHRISTIAN CAMPING*.

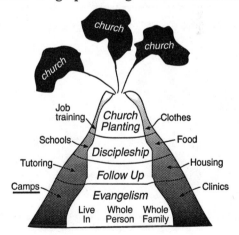

Between 60% and 70% of the decisions Christians make for salvation, rededication or vocational commitments (to become a missionary or minister) happen at retreats or camps.[6] These

6   David E. Klopfenstein, Dorothy A. Klopfenstein and George Williams, *Come Yourselves Apart: Christian Leadership in the Temporary Community* (Azusa, CA: Holysm Publishing, 1993), 4.

extended times away from our day-to-day routines impact us greatly.

The Lord gave us Morning Star Ranch in Kansas, THE OAKS in Southern California, Harmony Heart in the Poconos and Deer Creek in Colorado to supplement our urban outreach. Bible-club children love experiencing the wonders of God's creation. We employ teenagers who learn food preparation, service and clean up; gardening, maintenance, housekeeping and guest relations; and they teach young children about Christ by their lives and spoken words.

Virgil Gray spent two years at World Impact's Ranch in Kansas, gaining discipline and perspective. He recalls, "I rediscovered my walk with God there. My relationship had become routine. After that time of growth, I wanted to get back into the ministry and moved in to Watts."

Family camps are a highlight. A family vacation is out of the question for a single inner-city mother with several children. What would she do? Get on the bus and take her children where? Her options are often limited because of transportation, expense and job commitments. At our family camps, parents and their children enjoy a restful, peaceful, Christ-centered vacation.

One of my fondest memories of THE OAKS was watching a group of women, aged 25 to 35, splashing, laughing, screaming and enjoying themselves in the swimming pool one hot summer afternoon—recapturing their youth, which for many had been far too short. Their children were cared for by our staff, and these new believers loved their fellowship in Christ.

Another wonderful tradition, Christmas at THE OAKS, takes place on Saturdays in December. We encourage whole families to enjoy activities together which build Christmas memories. Adults and children play softball, decorate trees, make ornaments and go on hayrides *together*. Family portraits are taken and put in frames that the family members make. Later, many of these portraits become centerpieces of urban homes. Supporting churches serve many urban families their first sit-down meal.

After dinner, the families walk up an unlit path (it gets extremely dark at THE OAKS). Suddenly, a light appears and an angel announces, "Behold, I bring you great news. A Savior has been born!"

The excitement builds as the angel declares, "And He is a quarter of a mile down the road." The children run down the path, with the adults not far behind. As the families approach the nativity scene, they stand in amazement as the Christmas story is declared. Every year moms, dads, uncles and aunts hear the good news of Christmas—and a number accept Jesus as their Savior. The only downside to the day's events is that some children honestly believe that Jesus was born at THE OAKS!

Christian schools, job training and Christian camping are integral parts of our holistic ministry to the inner cities of America.

Addendum C

World Impact's Volcanic Church Planting

The volcano graphically pictures World Impact's dynamic ministry. A volcano has two separate, but complementary, parts.

1. The hot *inner core* is composed of evangelism, follow up, discipleship and church planting (World Impact's traditional ministries). In a volcano, pressure forces underground molten rock to the surface. Newly-planted churches explode out of the top of World Impact's inner core as the result of our dynamic in-depth ministry.

2. The structured *outer cone* includes housing, job training, food and clothing distribution, schools, camps and clinics (World Impact's structured, holistic ministries). In a volcano,

as pressure builds beneath the earth, and molten material is forced to the surface, a mountainous outer structure of rock and cinder forms around the hot inner core. Similarly, World Impact's outer-cone compassion ministries support (help, teach and equip) the new converts birthed out of our explosive, dynamic core ministries.

When the hot, molten core and the structured, outer cone function as a unit, many churches are planted (thrust out of the top of the volcano) even as others are being formed in its depths.

Without the hot inner core, the volcano becomes extinct, losing its dynamic nature and explosive potential. Spiritually, it resembles a fine organization that has lost its soul, i.e., Harvard University, founded by the Church but rendered a secular institution, content to educate the mind but not equip the spirit.

Without our structured outer-cone ministries, many new converts would fall away from Christ. A young person who is employed or attending one of our schools is more likely to resist the pull of the streets and remain faithful to Christ.

Active volcanoes often have several outlet spouts where pressure explodes through the outer cone. Hot molten material shot out the sides and top of Mt. St. Helens simultaneously, and volcanic ash spread all the way to our east coast. A church may be birthed out of a school, camp, clinic, sports league, thrift store or housing program. A Guatemalan-American church plant in Los Angeles might reproduce itself in Guatemala. The priority is to get the hot stuff (churches) into the world and not merely to build independent support structures, programs and institutions.

Differing Gifts

God uses people with differing gifts and temperaments to plant urban churches as the two parts of our volcano illustrate. Men and women involved in the inner core (church planters) are flexible and people-oriented. They gravitate toward dynamic, relational ministry. Outer-cone personnel are frequently more analytical and task-oriented, preferring the structured setting of institutional ministries. A team member's perspective of a situation depends on his responsibilities and personality.

Several women missionaries live in one of our staff homes. Hypothetically, one of these women might be a doctor, who works at our medical clinic in a structured setting from 8 a.m. to 5 p.m. each day. She rises two hours before she leaves for work to study and to spend time with the Lord. So she goes to bed at 9:00 p.m. Once she lies down she hears rowdy junior-high school students laughing, playing games and eating popcorn downstairs with her community-minister housemate. The doctor wishes these girls would be quiet so she could get a good night's rest. After all, she needs to be fresh to properly care for her patients the next day.

The following morning at 5 a.m. our physician gets up, exercises, reviews her new medical journals, eats breakfast, has devotions and precisely at 7:45 a.m. leaves for the clinic. She opens the doors exactly at 8 a.m. so her patients will not have to wait outside in the snow.

As the doctor leaves home that morning, she looks at the bedroom of her community-minister housemate and wonders why this woman is not up and serving the Lord. After all, godly people have their devotions *early* in the morning. While the doctor would never say it, she might quietly muse, "My housemate must be lazy, since she always sleeps in."

In contrast, the community minister watches the physician go to bed at 9:00 p.m., knowing that most ministry to junior- and senior-high aged girls takes place between 7:00 p.m. and midnight, and could wonder why the sleepyhead upstairs has forgotten that God called her to minister in the inner city.

Which woman do you want on your church-plant team? The answer is, "Both."

But in order to prevent Satan from having a heyday with petty jealousies, we need to communicate with each other about our respective responsibilities and how each helps to plant churches. The volcano cannot exist without both the inner core and the outer cone; healthy, thriving churches need both relational and structural ministries, which, in turn, need relational and structural church planters.

Addendum D

World Impact's Urban Institute

World Impact's Urban Institute equips inner-city pastors and lay people in the biblical basics for ministry, emphasizing how they can train their congregations. Zeal without biblical knowledge is dangerous. The Urban Institute has three distinctives:

First, The Urban Institute is ACCESSIBLE. It is affordable, culturally conducive (yet evangelical), relevant and geographically close. We bring biblical education to urban church workers.

Each *student* must be involved in lay or pastoral Christian leadership. The *learning group* is in a seminar setting, under the guidance of a mentor. The *mentor* helps individual students master the material, contribute and gain wisdom from the learning group, and develop ways to apply the learning in their context.[1]

Second, The Urban Institute is for URBAN MINISTRY. Our programs train urban Christians to minister among the urban poor.

Third, The Urban Institute concentrates on LEADERSHIP DEVELOPMENT. Our aim is to train a new generation of maturing inner-city pastors and lay people who will serve and equip God's people in the inner city.

For further information contact:
Dr. Don Davis, Director
The Urban Institute
3701 East 13th Street
Wichita, Kansas 67208
(316) 681-1317

---

[1] World Impact's Missionary Orientation Training Course (Los Angeles, CA: World Impact Press, 1996).

Addendum E

God's Standard For The Church Is Inclusiveness

"God was *reconciling* to Himself *everything* on earth and in heaven by the work of Christ when He made peace by His death on the Cross" (Colossians 1:20).[1]

Reconciling. Sinful man was reconciled to a holy God through Christ's sacrifice. God atoned for our sin (restored a relationship of harmony and unity between Himself and man) and appeased His own wrath. Peace and fellowship replaced hostility and alienation.[2]

Christians, reconciled to God, have been given the ministry of reconciliation. We are to encourage others to make peace with God, and then to be reconciled with their brothers and sisters. Reconciliation between God and man is the purpose of the gospel; it publicly demonstrates God's love (II Corinthians 5:18-20).

Everything. Christ's work reconciled everyone. "You are all sons of God through faith in Christ Jesus, for all of you who were baptized into Christ have clothed yourselves with Christ. There is neither Jew nor Greek, slave nor free, male nor female, for you are all one in Christ Jesus. If you belong to Christ, then you are Abraham's seed, and heirs according to the promise" (Galatians 3:26-29).

---

[1] See Isaiah 53:5 (The cost of reconciliation); Romans 5:10; Hebrews 2:17.
[2] *Nelson's Illustrated Bible Dictionary.* Nashville: Thomas Nelson Publishing, 1986), 903.

The Jew - Greek relationship refers to racial and cultural differences. Philip, a Jew, who baptized the Ethiopian eunuch,
preached to the Samaritans. The Jews hated the Samaritans
(John 4:9), calling them half-breeds, a mixture of Jewish and
Gentile blood. Philip's Samaritan ministry helped the Church
overcome its racial prejudice so it could become universal.

"For He Himself is our peace, who has made the two one
and has destroyed the barrier, the dividing wall of hostility, by
abolishing in His flesh the law with its commandments and
regulations. His purpose was to create in Himself *one new man*
(the Church) out of the two (Jews and Gentiles), thus making
peace" (Ephesians 2:14-16). The Church brought peace among
cultures that historically hated each other. Acts is a reconciliation story between Jews and Gentiles.

Christianity thrust Peter out of his cultural comfort zone.
Cornelius, a Gentile God-fearer attracted to the Jewish faith of
monotheism and morality, but not a committed proselyte (not
circumcised), saw a vision, followed God's instruction and sent
for Peter (Acts 10:18).

Peter, an orthodox Jew, had inherited prejudices against entering the home of a Gentile. It was against Jewish law to associate with or visit a Gentile. So God issued a special revelation
to Peter, "What God has cleansed is not unclean" (Acts 10:15),[3]
leading to Peter's confession, "God has shown me that I should
not call any man impure or unclean" (Acts 10:28). After obeying, Peter stated, "I now realize how true it is that God does not
show favoritism but accepts men from every nation who fear
Him and do what is right" (Acts 10:34-35). Cornelius was the
first person in the Roman world led to Christ under the apos-
tolic ministry (Acts 10:44). This act of inclusiveness paved the
way for future world evangelization.

There were at least 15 distinct cultures (language groups) at
the birth of the Church (Acts 2:9-11). Luke boasts that Jews
"from every nation under heaven" (Acts 2:5) were present in
Jerusalem. They became one in Christ.

---

[3] This declaration was foreshadowed by Jesus who had said, "It is not what man eats
that defiles him, but what comes out of a man's heart" (Mark 7:15-16).

The slave - free relationship refers to social and economic differences. Early Christians were socially and economically diverse: many were poor, slaves or former slaves.[4] Paul rejoiced that "not many wise men after the flesh, not many mighty, not many noble are called" (I Corinthians 1:26).

God frequently chose the poor (like Gideon), prostitutes (like Rahab), slaves (like Joseph) or shepherds (like David) to be rich in faith and to do His work. Yet some Christians in the first century had wealth, education and social prominence, and aided their less fortunate brothers.[5]

God left us on earth to do His will. Reconciliation is so important that Christ taught, "Before we can sacrifice (worship God) we first must be reconciled to our brothers" (Matthew 5:24). Even if reconciliation is costly, disciples of Jesus must obey.

---

[4] One quarter of the Roman Empire were slaves or former slaves. Lecture by Dr. Allan Callahan, Professor of New Testament at Harvard Divinity School at Westside Christian Fellowship, Santa Monica, California, 1996.

[5] Kenneth Scott Latourette, *A History of Christianity, Volume 1: Beginnings to 1500* (New York: Harper-Row, 1975), 80.

Addendum F

Your Involvement
with World Impact

For information on how you can become involved in World Impact's vital discipleship and church-planting ministry among the urban poor through prayer, financial support or as a volunteer or full-time staff member, write or call:

WORLD IMPACT, INC.   AREA CODE NOW
2001 S. Vermont Avenue   323
Los Angeles, CA 90007
Phone: (213) 735-1137 • Fax: (213) 735-2576
E-mail: info@worldimpact.org

Become Better Informed About World Impact Through:

Videos
Hope For The Inner City ($10).
A Celebration From The City ($10).

16mm Films
"When Hell Freezes Over"
"The Forgotten City"
"Why Bother?"
These three missionary movies are also available for purchase on one video cassette ($15).

Other Books By Dr. Phillips
They Dare To Love The Ghetto ($2).
The Making Of A Disciple ($5).
No Quick Fix ($5).

Videos, films and books are available from World Impact:
2001 S. Vermont Avenue, Los Angeles, CA 90007.

For Personal Involvement, Contact
World Impact Ministry Locations Directly:

Chester
700 Central Ave.
Chester, PA 19013
(610) 872-9220 office
(610) 499-9030 school

Dallas
4611 Samuell Blvd., Ste 161
Dallas, TX 75228
(214) 388-6405

Deer Creek Camp
228 S. Pine Dr.
Bailey, CO 80421
(303) 838-5647

Detroit
1062 Rademacher
Detroit, MI 48209
(313) 842-7188

Fresno
1955 Broadway St.
Fresno, CA 93721
(209) 442-0867

Harmony Heart Camp
RR 2, Box 246
Jermyn, PA 18433
(717) 254-6272

Los Angeles
2001 S. Vermont Ave.
Los Angeles, CA 90007
AREA CODE NOW 735-3400 office
323 (213) 735-2867 school

Newark
275 Sussex Ave.
Newark, NJ 07107
(201) 483-0326 office
(201) 483-3833 school

Oakland
P. O. Box 24452
Oakland, CA 94623
(510) 763-0352

THE OAKS
P. O. Box 437
Lake Hughes, CA 93532
(805) 724-1018

Morning Star Ranch
RR1, Box 13
Florence, KS 66851
(316) 274-4465

San Diego
1047 S. 39th St.
San Diego, CA 92113
(619) 263-3563

San Francisco
104 Sagamore St.
San Francisco, CA 94112
(415) 469-7494

St. Louis
3108 N. Grand Ave.
St. Louis, MO 63107
(314) 533-8313

Watts
2003 E. Imperial Hwy.
Los Angeles, CA 90059
(213) 566-6626 office
(213) 566-7154 school

Wichita
3701 E. 13th St.
Wichita, KS 67208
(316) 682-4075 office
(316) 681-1317 Urban Institute